# The Flight of Icarus

# Nigel Pearce

**chipmunkapublishing**
the mental health publisher

Published by
Chipmunkapublishing
United Kingdom

http://www.chipmunkapublishing.com

Copyright © Nigel Pearce 2016

ISBN 978-1-78382-277-5

About Chipmunkapublishing

Mental health books give a voice to writers with mental illness around the world. At Chipmunkapublishing we raise awareness of mental health and the stigma surrounding mental health problems by encouraging society to listen. We are documenting mental health literature as a genre so history does not forget the survivors and carers of people with mental illness and disabilities.

**Mental Health Biography**

Born in 1959 into a dysfunctional, although outwardly functioning family in some ways, in that our parents looked like members of 'the new middle class' but they had no friends. Four people maimed by circumstances and possibly inherent instability. He was intellectually advanced for his years, which created frictions and anomalies. Nigel quickly gravitated towards avant-garde people and revolutionaries. Running away to London, where he would meet a variety of people in the early 1970's as a child. A combination of misfortune, mind-bending drugs and mental ill health caused him to be taken into the care of the County Council, fostered by academics, and admission to psychiatric hospitals. In 1986 while in one of those rambling old asylums he began a systematic studying with The Open University graduating with a B.A. (Hons) 2:1. He then became seriously physically ill as a consequence of over-medication and also some neglect. Almost died at Christmas 2003; he had been, it was to become apparent, 'toxic' for a protracted period. The doctors abandoned any hope and it looked like 'care' in institutions for the rest of his life. Fighting back, he persuaded the doctors to let him return to his flat. They had said 'you will never study again.' Since then he has gained a Certificate in English Studies at Warwick University, a Diploma of Higher Education, a Diploma of Higher Education in Humanities and a BA. (Hons) Humanities with Creative Writing 2:1 all at The Open University and hopes to begin the Creative Writing M.A in the autumn. He is the proud author of eight books with Chipmunkapublishing. A doctor, a G.P., said to him last week: 'The Open University and Chipmunkapublishing saved your life.'

## Book Description

This is my second hardback with Chipmunkapublishing. It is an attempt to create thematic continuity within a generic division into memoir, prose-fiction and poetry. However, as is the tendency with memoir in the postmodern epoch it is fragmented.

> People often suggest that the future of biography lies in a radical change of form - in the development of fractured or post-modern narrative models. But this has been going on for quite a time.

Cline and Angier (2014) *Life Writing: A Writers & Readers* Companion. p. 118.

Having said that all the material of whatever genre has a material base in 'lived experience', but it is also the work of a creative mind. Therefore, it is for the reader to engage. For as Jean-Paul Sartre argued in *What is Literature*'

> The dialectic is nowhere more apparent than in the
> art of writing for the literary object is a peculiar top
> this exists only in movement. To make it come
> into view a concrete act called reading is necessary,
> and it lasts only as this act lasts. Beyond that, there are
> only black marks on paper.

> - Sartre (2010) *What is Literature*, p. 29

4

The Flight of Icarus

**Part one**

**A memoir in its socio-cultural context.**

**One Beginning.**

> He who controls the past controls the future, and he
> who controls the present controls the past.

**-George Orwell**.

'The social revolution cannot take its poetry from the past,

but only the future.'

**- Karl Marx.**

Surfacing from a dark ocean of sleep, I heard the ghostly voice of my father calling out from the worm gnawed Beyond:

'Nigel, Nigel.'

Surely a dream, but no a hallucination for I threw myself out of sleep into an alert consciousness. However, the voice came from my urn which contained the remnants of both my parent's ashes. It would be a day of bizarre coincidences and narrow escapes. The old boy had forewarned of the potential calamitous events during that day, and they were unpleasant, but could have been much worse, Nevertheless, it created a need, the requirement to reassess, although I don't want to use the language of French Existentialism one is compelled to tell things truthfully. I experienced an 'existential crisis' and knew Albert Camus had said in *The Myth of Sisyphus*:

The consequences of realization are suicide or recovery.

Albert Camus, *The Myth of Sisyphus*.

Recovery for people like me is equated with writing. Hence this manuscript is carved out of my memory, heart and brain. I have attempted to let people speak for themselves and the quotes are verbatim, or at least as is reasonable to expect.

The Flight of Icarus

I had no idea of where I came from when young as a child. Only was aware of what I was fleeing until much older and then could apply Reason and achieve a forgiveness of sorts begotten by an understanding. Much had been inculcated in me. It was rather like a youthful tattoo which wore off with time. The problem was as a little boy I had absolutely no intention of tattooing myself. Indeed, I didn't, but there were people who had interests in impregnating my mind, patterning my brain into waves which were generated from their transmitters. These curved the waves of my thinking so decisively that I would only discover the freedom of a kind upon their demise. I took absolutely no pleasure in their deaths. Indeed, I was shaken to my core. These people were not the revolutionaries, psychiatrists, social workers or the druggists who my family blamed for my decline into madness and swings of mood. Basically anyone other than themselves These people were tragically the members of my family: three emotional cripples, not bad people, but profoundly emotionally damaged for one or more reasons. There was also a history of mental instability on both sides of that family. However, that is not to suggest the drug enhanced exploration of my psyche which began at the age of twelve was etched in stone at the beginning of Time; it was not pre-destined and played a role in the mayhem which would engulf me. Neither was my descent into insanity pre-ordained, I am not a biological reductionist, although my goodness I have met a lot of them. I do like Foucault *Madness and Civilisation* believe 'madness' is socially constructed.

I am now 56 and have some knowledge of why they blurted out such venom and at times nonsense, those damaging vibrations, threats and histrionics. All three were the products of their time and therefore rooted in the dialectic of History which is one of the conflicting and dynamic relationship between individual agency and social-cultural forces.

7

To quote Marx:

> Man makes his own history, but he does not make it out
>
> of the whole cloth; he does not make it out of conditions
>
> chosen by himself, but out of such as he finds close at hand.
>
> - Karl Marx, *The Eighteenth Brumaire of Louis Bonaparte.*

But let me begin at wherever it all began, or at least at one conjuncture. When my biological father realized I was reading Marx, Lenin, Mao and Bobby Seale, the Black Panther, at the age of eleven, I was deeply engrossed and my 'world-view' had changed, but I was also reading Dylan Thomas *Under Milk Wood* and *Selected Poems* as well as Albert Camus *The Fall*. I had decided like Camus' character Jean-Baptiste Clamence to wander and then tell my tale as a "judge-penitent.' My father had other ideas to mine though, although he was aware of the benefits of education:

> 'You will never learn all you need to know from books. You
>
> will need experience of the world.''

The method of Marxist 'praxis' had been unwittingly affirmed by my father as was a youthful relating to Jean-Baptiste Clamence from Camus' novel. Since I had read:

> The philosophers have interpreted the world, the point is,
>
> however, to change it
>
> - Karl Marx, *Eleventh Thesis on Feuerbach.*

However, this is not the source of the flight of Icarus although I believed it to be at the time. Its origins were in two people who lived through The Great Depression of the 1930's as children, both were indelibly marked by this and the inhuman horrors of war on a scale later generations could not comprehend, 50,000,000 people died, 26,000,000 from the Soviet Union and over 6 million in the Nazi attempt to 'purge humanity' of every human type accept Aryan, but including no Aryan homosexuals, mentally ill in anyway or communists and there was also an industrial attempt to eliminate European Jewry known as 'The Final Solution.' The Second World War really was an existential threat to humanity.

My father's past was shrouded in the mists of nebula until he was very old. There had been a rumour that he had run away to sea at 14.Then as I studied for my first degree at The Open University and read about 'battle fatigue' which is what doctors called Post Traumatic Stress Disorder in Second World War soldiers he told me his story, or at least parts of it. But who isn't self-censoring? My mother was a literary and creative character who was ill fitted for the rigors of the nuclear family. Really neither of them was temperamentally orientated to the prison of the family. I would learn, early from my mother, and much later from my father that the 'families' they grew up in were less than an adequate apparatus for the socialization of the next generation of parents.

Herr Dad, as I called him when ill, had come from quite a privileged Yorkshire family. Holidaying in Malta when he was a child he fell down the steps of Malta, banged his head and wore thick glasses for the rest of his life. Did this explain his rages? I would never know and either will anyone else. But I did glean his father was an architect in the Royal Engineers, posted to Shanghai when dad was about 14 and my paternal grandmother whom I never met refused to go. You could not be a single mother in Yorkshire in the 1930s. Dad headed for London, became a rough sleeper on The Embankment, did illegal work washing-up in hotels where he would be fed and given enough money to knock him out for the night with alcohol. It was around about 1934 when father joined the Communist Party of Great Britain. Possibly a tactical move, but he was sponsored by the Party, or at least an individual within it, to do his General Certificate of Education and rent a room in run down 'digs'. He swept through studying relentlessly as if his life depended on it. He travelled back North to Leeds Infirmary and won the National Silver Medal for Nursing. There he met a medical student who dad seems to have confided in: the diagnosis this junior doctor made was 'paranoid schizophrenia'. Dad would have known what happened to psychiatric patients in the 1930's. You were admitted and that was that, you did not get out. I do not believe he ever told Mater, my mum, but he lived with that diagnosis correct or not for the rest of his life self-medicating with alcohol and sleeping tablets. However, Dad would move rightwards, but that was later.

1936 was a significant year for that generation: The Spanish Civil War or 'The Poets War' as it became known because so many writers went to fight fascism and defend the Republic in Spain began. So did the Moscow Show Trials with Stalin eliminating the old Bolshevik leadership. My father's best friend in the Communist Party of Great Britain joined the International Brigades and went to Spain to fight, dad told me he thought this was a 'sideshow' and the fight would be with Nazi Germany. I do not know if dad left or was expelled from the Communist Party. However, he related a story to me of how in 1937 he had read in the *Daily* Worker about Bukharin's trial and his public 'confessions' and just didn't believe what he was reading. Anyway, he left the Communist Party and spent a short period as a District Nurse in a deprived part of Glasgow before joining the Royal Army Medical Corps in early 1938. The clouds of war were gathering. I believe that he really did have illusions in the U.S.S.R as the C.P.G.P's internal education programme was very efficient. He could never accept the validity of any Trotskyist position; it would have been programmed out of him in the Communist Party of Great Britain. This would have profound ramifications for my relationship with him as I joined a neo-Trotskyist group when very young. There was also a tendency in the C.P.G.P to see

Trotskyists as intellectuals with no base in the working class and or as declassed students or Bohemians .

He was by this time quite dependent on the booze, what soldiers came to call in later generations "squaddie medicine.' Dad does seem to have had a rebellious streak as the following tale delineates. He used to tell this one with his favourite tumbler of whisky taken neat in his hand:

> "One day at Aldershot barricades my mate and I hot-wired the
> Commanding Officer's car and went on a two day binge. We were
> so drunk, we drove it straight back into his parking space. I was
> given the choice: forty-eight hours in the glasshouse [military
> prison] without cigarettes or twenty-four hours on the assault course
> with smokes. I did the assault course.'

Total War in Europe began in September 1939; there was a war-fever, but not like World War 1. Many of the working class people who went to fight were ideologically motivated. They were fighting against fascism rather than for 'King and Country'. However, there were nasty incidents in London though when the poet and pacifist Dylan Thomas registered as 'conscientious objector'; they were called "conchies' by the mob, he was beaten-up very badly. You will possibly have noted by now there is not an emotional dimension in this part of father's life. This is simply because there was not one, as far as I am aware, he was emotionally paralysed, it was about survival and those other elements of being down and out, fighting back up and then being capitulated into industrial war. Dad was to find what a lot of soldiers discover in the army, both camaraderie and something akin to a home. All be it the house of the dead and death.

In 1939 father was sent with the British Expeditionary Force to France. However, the Nazi tactic of fast armoured war with close air support known as Blitzkrieg was an innovation in military tactics. The French had built a static defence called the Maginot Line; the light armoured German divisions simply outflanked it. The French army was routed, leaving a small British army exposed to ferocious attack. They carried out a retreat to Dunkirk in 1940 where an armada of military and civilian craft shipped the majority back to Britain. Many were mowed down by fighter-bombers on the beaches and wading in the water. My father's little group of men was cut off from the general retreat to Dunkirk being compelled to move southwards. Here was Vichy France with many fascist sympathizers.  It was during this retreat that dad had the following experience:

"Twenty or so of us were heading for the coast further south. We were spotted by a Junkers Ju 87, a Stuka Dive Bomber. The only shelter in the exposed countryside was a barn in which we hid. He strafed this barn for an hour. Just again and again. They were armour piercing rounds. I saw my mates torn apart. About seven of us were lucky enough to make it."

The only conclusion I could draw was the pilot was intoxicated by a blood-lust. They could have been no military objective in strafing a barn with retreating infantrymen in for an hour. I was beginning to understand that irrational acts are committed in war. The survivors headed further South to a fishing village, luck was on their side and this village was sympathetic not to Vichy France, but the allies. A small fishing boat took dad and his six comrades across the English Channel. Britain stood alone against the formidable Nazi war machine until 1941 when the Soviet Union entered the war against Nazism.

He seems to have had little respite and was sent to North Africa in 1941 to fight. I know little of this except for three remarks. They were very revealing. Firstly, father told me:

> 'There is nothing worse than desert warfare; it is the boredom, just
> the interminable boredom.'

As to illustrate the consequences of previous rational and, presumably, not sadistic men and his own triumph over the irrational and ethical supremacy he would relate this episode:

> 'Men would get Jerry cans [petrol cans] and pour enough petrol around
> a scorpion to make it begin stringing itself to death, but I did not do any
> thing like that. I played endless games of chess on an old set with a friend.'

It strikes me that he only played chess with me two or three times. Perhaps he did not like losing. He managed to miss the Battle of El Aleman, but saw action at both Sieges of Tobruk. Stitching the narrative together a decline can be perceived. At Tobruk there were only a few hundred yards separating the lines, both dug in and it became apparent that dad was taking unnecessary chances:

> 'I didn't care; I would put my head above the parapet. Once a German
> sniper spotted me. I heard the report of his rifle and almost simultaneously
> someone pulled me down; the bullet just grazed my head.'

By 1943 he had volunteered and was training for a General Wingate's guerrilla mission behind Japanese lines in Burma which took place between 1943 and 1944. I did some research, Wingate was a manic-depressive and it was obvious the Chindit offensive would have no appreciable effect on the Allied war-effort. I tentatively mentioned this to my father who I had known caught Malaria during the mission and an Australian soldier, risking 'court-marshal', had carried him on his back through the

Burmese jungle. Then I read that the Chindits were given Malaria jabs. I plucked up courage on one drunken night; every night was for dad:

'Dad, why didn't you have the Malaria jab in Burma?'

'I didn't care; I just wasn't bothered what happened to me.'

I never pursued it beyond that. You just did not with him that was something I learnt very young. Instead, I asked about General Wingate:

'He was mad Nigel, totally insane.'

'Sometimes troubled men achieve positions of leadership in wars.' I replied diplomatically.

His memories of Burma, suppressed and those repressed, would haunt him throughout his life. He told me little, but I would hear him screaming in his nightly alcohol and Nitrazepam induced stupors. One memory, he did relate on a regular basis was how he and the others guerrillas had to hack and carve out the leeches from their flesh in the Burmese jungle. Also a sense of betrayal because some of the Burmese population was sympathetic to the Japanese hoping that a British defeat would bring about the collapse of the British Empire in the East. Apparently informants had notified the Japanese about certain 'drop-zones.' Many Chindits were sent into the jungle in lightweight plywood gliders, sharpened bamboo stakes would have torn these flimsy aircraft apart and mutilated the men inside. War is no romantic drama, I can tell you, and it destroys millions and leaves generations maimed in its bloody wake. His feeling regarding the Chindits was doubtless compounded by the Malaria, he was in a coma for six weeks and there can be little doubt his mental health was by this time in tatters.

However, industrial-scale war is not just a parasite it is a predatory and by 1945 he was back in Europe as Nazi Germany was on the verge of military defeat. I hadn't

14

known, but there were small 'labour-camps' dotted across Europe. As the fascists retreated, they left an inhumane havoc. I had asked further about the so-called concept of victimhood of those rounded up and transported to slave-labour or extermination camps. He simply described the following:

'First the sappers had to go into de-electrify the outer boundary fence,

then clear the mines and finally smash away in for the medics. The

Germans had just left piles of corpses, rotting and covered in lice.

We used D.D.T to kill the insects. Most of the naked and emaciated

bodies were goners. Those that weren't, there was little you could do

just attempt to hydrate them, intravenously, anyway, it was hopeless.'

There his narrative about World War 11 ended, it never went beyond that point. Once I asked him:

'Dad, did you kill men during the war'

'You don't ask old soldiers that.'

I had no experience of violence on that scale or I would not have asked.

How father, my biological one, would have developed psychologically without his experiences during the Great Depression of the 1930's and the Second World War I will never know. What I do know was something profound within him was wrong, perhaps that medical student was partially correct in his diagnosis at Leeds Infirmary. I had little contact with him while he was in the army. This was much later during the Cold War, in the Army of The Rhine in West Germany. He was out all day running the Pharmacy and down at the Mess [a mess is an area where military personnel socialize, eat, and drink at subsidised rates] every night getting drunk. I was always in bed when he returned so I just don't know if or how erratic his behaviour was at that juncture. My mum persuaded him to leave the Army after twenty-one years when I was just coming up to five. She refused to allow me to interact with the other children on the base, indeed with anyone. However, an early memory lingers from the British base in Düsseldorf. The mother was cleaning the quarters, the house, which had large, heavy ceramic lamp shades, like huge frozen teardrops. Mum was clearing one while standing on a chair. Somehow it smashed and there was blood everywhere. At the age of three you know an emergency when you see one. Fortunately, I managed to shift the front door open and another army wife heard my cries for help. She took me to her home and mum was rushed to the barracks hospital. It was quite a shock. Nevertheless, I was soon at home with mother again, she had no friends. I think the reality was I was mum's only friend, at least until she retired and a tragic but lucrative inheritance made her think again. He was transformed from a monster:

> 'The biggest mistake of my life was marrying him', 'that Victorian
> Patriarch', 'a brute.'

She regularly said until the metamorphosis when he became the light of her life referred to as 'old faithful'. From blazing rows since, at least, I was about six via Marriage Guidance Counselling a couple of years later to mum having to get a job in 1969 as a clerical worker to make sure the supply of food was maintained. The catalyst for this was mum used to receive 'housekeeping' and there was only one tin of Heinz Tomato soup left. I said mum could have it; mum heated it up for me. He was having one of his attacks and had refused to give her any further finance. But hey presto, decades later they have money and are compelled to either 'sink or swim' when they retired and suddenly the Party 'line' changed too:

> 'We have the perfect relationship.'

Amazing what money and necessity can do, especially when it was about your own survival. If I was staying at theirs in the post-conflict period and I wanted to go to the toilet during the night I was expected to apologise in the morning just in case I woke him up. The absurdity of it ached into a huge vacuum of nothingness when mother, Mater, started peeling grapes for Herr Dad. It was quite literally a dialectical leap or more a descent on her part into total submission and passivity. I had seen her, when a young child, one night as he was berserk throwing the clothes she had bought him with the 'housing keeping' allowance yelling they were too 'flamboyant' confronts him in the Southpaw boxing stance and she said:

'Come on then, fight.'

To his credit, he realized how bizarre this was having boxed regularly in army gyms and calmed down.

**An essay about the 1930's, particularly the International Brigades in Spain.**

They read Marx. They became communists; they became anti-fascists.

**Virginia Woolf.**

Communism in the truest sense is an effort to think, and then into action,

human society as an organism (not a machine which is too static a

Metaphor).

**Louis MacNeice.**

I I shall argue that a dialectical tension existed between Woolf's understanding of the aesthetic nature of poetry which was essentially a *Victorian poetic* which I argue is flawed. However it is an aestheticism view and was contradicted by the complexified literary method presented by many writers of W. H. Auden's generation as illustrated in Christopher Caudwell *Illusion and Reality* (1937), which I favour, and Auden *Introduction to the Penguin Book of Light Verse* (1938) who developed to a greater and lesser degree respectively a dialectical materialist view of British poetry. I shall show that in Skelton's anthology *Poetry of The Thirties (*2000) Auden *Spain (c. 1937)* wrote a complexified poetics consistent with this literary methodology. However, this cannot as Woolf argues, is separated from the work of T. S. Eliot. Indeed, it is contextualized by the Modernist poetry of Eliot (1919) *Prufrock and Other Observations* and also in his masterpiece *The Wasteland* in 1922. However I also maintain that because of the material contradictions of Modernity and the 'reflection' of this in literature created in the iconic writer of modernist poetry, T.S. Eliot, a contradictory consciousness in his literary output. This can be perceived in the tensions between his revolutionary stylistic innovations and his 'conservative' literary criticism even before his shift to Anglo-Catholicism. These can be comprehended in the context of contradictory and contending Modernisms reflected by the material contradictions into the ideological 'superstructure'. This contestation between the old and new productive forces in a period of social transformation can be manifested as fragmentation of the consciousness which can be seen in Eliot which mirrored the crisis of post WW1 European capitalism. The revolutionary and the reactionary forces which emanated from the material conditions contented for hegemonic cultural dominance. The methodology I employ in this analysis was encapsulated initially by Marx in the Preface to *A Contribution to the Critique of Political Economy* (1859):

> In the social production of their life, men enter into definite
> relations that are indispensable and independent of their will,
> relations of production which correspond to a definite stage of
> development of their material forces...The mode of production
> conditions the social, political and intellectual life process in general.'

Marx.

The creation of a new mode of production, which developed into finance capitalism unleashing yet more competing social and economic classes but also contending models of literary production. This upheaval was characterized in Lenin (1916) *Imperialism, The Highest Stage of Capitalism* as 'moribund capitalism'. It is the crisis of modern in which he also described as 'late capitalism'. Ernst Fischer in *The Necessity of Art: a Marxist Approach* (1978) applies this pertinent to the art:

> In a decaying society, art, if it is to be truthful, must also reflect
> decay. And unless it wants to break faith with its social function,
> art must show the world as changeable.'

Fischer (1978) p. 48.

The European 'Mind' was not the homogenised entity claimed by Eliot in *Tradition and Individual Talent* (1919) with its individual traditions, it was a system torn by war and crisis:

> The whole of the literature of Europe from Homer and
> within it the whole of the literature of his own country has
> a simultaneous order. This historical sense which is timeless
> as well as temporal.

Eliot (1919)

The revolutionary nature of *Prufrock and Other Observations* (1917) which in there form and content challenged the hegemony of the bourgeoisie which he was paradoxically defending in his conservative criticism. T.S.Eliot was the personification of the contradiction of literature in 'late-capitalism': both avant-garde yet reactionary. The writers of the 1930's were caught between these opposing forces. However, many did not sit on or lean against an ivory tower as Woolf had argued, but volunteered with the International Brigades or the more independent P.O.U.M. to fight Fascism in the Spanish Civil War as Orwell in *Homage to Catalonia* (1938) illustrates vividly . Some of the writers Woolf critiques in *The Leaning Tower* (1940) did as she points out:

> They feel compelled to preach, if not by their living, at least by
> their writing, the creation of a society in which everyone is equal
> and everyone is free. It explains the pedagogic, the didactic, the
> loud-speaker strain of their poetry.

Woolf

Auden   had articulated in these words the milieu which many of these writers inhabited included a belief that it was necessary to transform the 'means of production' in order to solve the malady of the estrangement of literary production, in particular that of the poet:

> In such a society it, and, in such alone, will it be possible for the
> poet, without   sacrificing any of the subtleties or his integrity, to
> write poetry which is simple, clear and gay.
> For poetry which is at the same time light and adult can only be
> written in a society which is both integrated and free

> Auden

Eliot had maintained in *The Perfect Critic* (1920) that:

> The creative writer and citric should frequently be the same person.

> Eliot.

Here Eliot is undermining the very position he articulated as the theory of the 'depersonalized poet', the poet cannot, I would maintain, be both an anonymous 'poet persona' and then self-consciously create a body of criticism about this work. These inconsistencies in Eliot are at the heart of his project for creating a *modern classicist poetics*. The conflicts, contestation and ambiguities are thus evident in Woolf's essay *The Leaning Tower* for three reasons, firstly Woolf's understanding of Romanticism is flawed in that she does not comprehend the revolutionary nature of *Preface* to Lyrical Ballads written by Wordsworth in 1802  which rather than positing the solitary aesthete of Woolf's essay he wrote:

> The principal object, then, which I proposed to myself in
> these Poems was to choose incidents and situations from
> common life, and to relate or describe them, throughout,

as far as was possible, in a selection of language really

used by men.

Wordsworth.

In its context at a time of revolutionary tumult by contesting Classicism as the dominant verse form is was radical as opposed to conservative. Secondly when she wrote *The Leaning Tower* the USSR were not supporting Britain, they only did so later so in that context I would argue some of the comments about Leftist poet 'winning' and 'bleating' against the system that educated them is unbecoming of a great woman of letters and finally she does not anticipate David Hume's philosophical critique of her version of the why do you stay argument , ''a society which would like to kick them off its back' Virginia Woolf where Hume likened dissenters to captives on a ship who were unable to get off (Hume 1748). In opposition to Auden, who in *Memory of W.B. Yeats* (1939) wrote 'poetry makes nothing happen' .I would argue following Bertolt Brecht

Art is not a mirror to reflect reality,

Rather it is a hammer to shape it

Brecht, (1982)

I shall use a 'close reading' of Auden, Spain to make my argument.  I agree with Caudwell in his exposition of the essential feature regarding the social nature of Art:

Art has social functions. This is not a Marxist demand

but arises from the very way art forms are defined. Only

those things that are recognized as art forms which have

a conscious social function.

Caudwell.

My 'close-reading' which illustrates my thesis is Auden, *Spain (c. 1937)*, I adhere to Caudwell's insight regarding the general writing of poetry, Auden and the Audenesque in in the 1930's when he wrote:

> But a prerequisite is to attain a world-view that will become
>
> general...This Auden, Spender and Lewis have so far failed
>
> to do.

Caudwell.

That is they didn't embrace and understand the methodology of dialectical materialism and hence their later Rightward turn. Auden *Spain* (c, 1937). Auden would in 1965 refer to this poem 'as a bad influence' thus retrospectively editing his work, at least in ideological term. But Auden is not here writing a simplistic didactic poem. The 'force' of his 'foregrounding' of the signifiers 'yesterday', 'today' and tomorrow' for the 'signified 'History'. He uses these refrains in a particular synaptic pattern throughout the poem to create a sense both the immediacy of the Spanish Civil War and the larger overarching context of human history. He juxtaposes the old 'Yesterday' in which Medieval and Romantic are represented by two troupes as follows and contrasted with the urgency of Spain:

> Yesterday the prayer at sunset
>
> And the adoration of the madman. But today the struggle

Auden.

We can also see his use of assonance to stress both the contrast, but also, paradoxically the continuity of paradigmatic model: with the 'ya' of 'Yesterday' and ay of 'prayer' and the 'ae' of 'Sunset'. The controversial nature of phrases like:

> ...the young poets exploding like bombs'

Auden.

Is to an extent overemphasised as it is a simile used as a poetic device, and therefore means 'exploding with ideas' as well as an encouragement to join the International Brigades

And

The conscious acceptance of guilt in the necessary murder:

Auden

Here Auden is writing as much the Freudian psychoanalytical poet as the recruiting sergeant. So hens he makes 'conscious the 'necessary Oedipus or Elektra Complex as a poetic Bildungsroman or 'coming of age' Orwell is missing the point in regard of poetry here, I would suggest::

So much of this sort of left-wing thought of playing with fire

by people who don't even know the fire is hot.

Orwell

It is apparent from this couplet which forms the end of a quatrain and his use of alliteration and metaphor

History the operator, the

Organizer, Time the refreshing river.

Auden.

The 'o's reinforce the agency and 'world-historic mission' to coin Fredrick Engels phrase of the proletariat with the poetic mode of the post-revolutionary 'refreshing river.' However the enjambment: the/Organizer is a little dissonant and suggests a wariness of the 'Party organizer.' We can understand Auden's poem not as a crude piece of didactic writing, but a complicated and well-constructed piece of verse. Obviously he was in favour of the International Brigades, but this is poetry not sloganizing. Indeed, it is only by the proletariat acting as the agent of social transformation, can we have a 'new' poetry:

> The social revolution...cannot draw poetry from the past,
>
> only the future.
>
> Marx

**World War 11, the 1930's the other Story.**

My mother spent the Second World War in the village of her birth, Longfield in Kent. As a teenage girl she listened to both the *Home Service* for news of the War and the *Third Programme* where she fell in love with the music of Beethoven played by the brilliant Jewish violin virtuoso Yehudi Menuhin and an émigré Hungarian pianist named simply Solomon. She attempted to aid the 'war-effort' by becoming a Land Girl, a member of the Women's Land Army (WLA), but two nights of 'slumming it' was enough for mum and she returned home. Also she avoided those 'course American G. I's' who were stationed nearby before D-Day, the Normandy Landings in 1944. Home was not a happy place, though. This I learnt when very young. Here there had been another fall involving a man, her father who drunk away his string of Blacksmith businesses while 'making Nan have seven children.' He either died prematurely of drink or went his own way, I was never told. Her sisters had moved to Battersea where they endured the Blitz of 1940 and Doodlebug V.1 unmanned rockets of 1944 and later in 1945 the larger V. 2's. Mum as the youngest remained at home. The brothers did not see 'active service', but Frank and Reg as well as Doris joined the Communist Party of Great Britain after the war because of the sacrifices made by the Soviet Union [Russian] during the War. Frank dropped-out, Reg left in protest at the U.S.S.R's intervention in the Hungarian Revolution of 1956 and Doris after being knocked to the ground by a rather large police horse on a demonstration in the late-1950's. Doris did not have the confidence to return to the CPGB. She would later spend a year in a psychiatric hospital. One sister was known as Pickle because of her bewildering ways. Pickle was not visited often, well, none of them were.My parents went to 'a show' in the West End so I stayed with her. It was really great though and we stayed up talking far too late and got into trouble. Pickle and I.

**Brief Encounter.**

There was a post-war romance on mum's side. In 1946, she decided to spread her wings a little and there was the question of money as well. Mum enrolled at the Pitman's Secretarial College in London. British Army veterans were given grants and access to university on a privileged basis. Mum met one, I was never told his name, in London. He 'fell' totally for mum and they shared an interest in classical music and serious literature, the 'classics of literature', not the avant-grade material which had been flowing from the pens of Jean-Paul Sartre and Albert Camus. There was the new nationalized train service between London and Dartford and then a short bus journey home to Longfield. This chap started taking mum to venues like the Albert Hall to concerts, but mum always had to leave early to catch the train home. Undeterred, he saved up and bought a second hand car to drive out to Kent at the weekends. Mum 'turned him down'. From what I could gather he had made a proposal of marriage. Then no information was forthcoming until something happened in 1952. My sister was born, our parents were married. We were not told how they met, but once I asked father if he had 'girlfriends' before he met mum. He just glared at me.

### Births, accidents and inadequacy

My sister, seven years my senior may or may not have been planned. Seven years passed and a volcanic eruption sent the family into crises. I came along unplanned and mum could not cope with a young daughter and a newborn son. She was sent away to St. Hilary's Preparatory School in Godalming as a 'boarder'. Recall father was in The Army of The Rhine, hence in West Germany. So my sister was sent to boarding school in another country at the age of seven having been informed by an infertile sister of mum's that her mother couldn't cope with her. Here was the detonator and the wiring for the munitions left by the Great Depression of the 1930's and World War 2. She would be contorted with hatred and consumed with anger for the rest of her life. When she returned from St. Hillarys at 11, dad had left the Royal Army Medical Corps and retrained in Environmental Nursing. Basically, he entered Fords massive Dagenham Car plant to help run the factory, yes, ensure profits, but also to keep the men and women safe from danger. It was a mighty step for dad to leave his 'home' which was The Army. He became 'management' at Fords and didn't mum know it. He had an army friend, but Farap was now 'too vulgar' for the dad to associate with. I hate to say it, but mum was a little bit of a snob. I really don't know where these attitudes emanated from with two of her brothers and a sister in the Communist Party of Britain. Mum was still isolated except for me and dad had to drink at home in whisky sodden solitude. This bifurcation between the children caused immense harm. My sister was 'offered' a leucotomy upon her first admission to the Maudsley which she refused, but went to the Bethlem Community for therapy instead. This 'fault-line' was possibly the one which caused the earthquake from which an enormous amount of really profound and irrevocable damage occurred. She would wreak revenge and I am of the opinion it was committed unconsciously.

**The Summer of Love (1967) versus 'The Fear Pit' and beyond.**

Timothy Leary's advice to my sister's generation was simple yet complex, people really did take the whole 'counterculture' scene very seriously. He said to them:

Turn on, tune in and drop out.

Or to quote him to better effect than this mere slogan:

Like every great religion of the past we seek to find the

divinity within and to express this revelation in a life of glorification

and the worship of God. These ancient goals we define in the metaphor

of the present — turn on, tune in, drop out.

This entailed the use of L.S.D for the purposes of self-discovery and exploration of the mind, both conscious and unconscious, and other dimensions. Leary heralded it:

An ontological awakening.

The average dose of Lysergic acid diethylamide or L.S.D-25 was in 1967 around two to three times more potent than it was during by the 1980's, but people were not taking it or any else much else just for 'kicks'. The 'counterculture' was **not** primarily about Hedonism although it was about emancipation and also 'the death-trip'. There was a strong tendency of what Freud thought to be the life-force Eros, love, but this was mirrored by an undercurrent of Thanatos, the death wish. Also the New Left was interacting with and within the 'counter-culture' and there were experiments in communal living without power hierarchies and with 'free love'. With the use of hallucinogenic drugs came a 'turn to the East spiritually' in the 'scene' with some using Transcendental Meditation and the growth of the Krishna Consciousness or 'Hare Krishna' movement and these renounced the use of drugs in favour of meditation induced, chant orientated: 'out of the body, space travel', I must say I knew a lot of 'acid' or L.S.D casualties and people with 'speed', amphetamine, psychosis who became 'mystics' as well as many people looking for a route out of opioid addiction. L.S.D was used in its earliest days with alcoholics and anti-psychiatry doctors like R. D. Laing and David Cooper believed in its beneficial properties. As an antidote about its use during the 1960's I recall this conversation with the Nursing Officer, Mr. Lewis, at the Regional Adolescent Unit in 1974

'I can absolutely understand why you take it Nigel. I have also

under laboratory conditions. It opened my mind and I remember

hearing colours and seeing sounds. It was beautiful.'

An essential part of the counter-culture was Timothy Leary suggested:

That life should be lived as art.

My sister met and fell in love with a young man, this was before the Dangerous Drugs Act 1969, when people with opioid addiction were prescribed pharmaceutical heroin by doctors or 'croakers' as they were known to the addicts. He introduced her to it and a whole spectrum of illicitly obtained mind-altering substances. It should be pointed out that the counterculture was a movement of disenchanted and utopian largely young and middle-class people. This is not to say the masses were not radicalized by the anti-Vietnam War movement, the 'Cultural Revolution' of Maoism, student activism, Radical Feminism, the beginning of the Gay Liberation Front and the Black Panther Party. It was generally a period of experimentation both social and individual and it really became generalized in 1967, the summer is known as the Summer of Love. By the spring of 1968 students and workers were in control of

Prague although the U.S.S.R would military intervene to crush 'the Prague Spring'. I found this confused a seven year old. Why should a State that purports to be Socialist go around pacifying a revolution which was given the buzz phrase 'the human face of socialism.' I did not find the answers until I met university students and a PhD at the local university who belonged to a neo-Trotskyist organization just after my eleventh birthday. Also, it seemed fairly obvious the mass Moscow based Communist Party has 'sold out' the French Revolution of May 1968 during which the barricades went up in Paris under the influence of the Situationalists, Trotskyists and Maoists. My first endeavours were to look to Maoism like an awful of people did in the late 1960's and early 1970's. I was much impressed by Mao's writings, in the West we knew little, at that time, of the excesses of the 'Cultural Revolution' and the 'Red Guards'. Here are three examples which I recall capturing my imagination, indeed my heart. Recall that at this time the Vietnam War was being waged. A group of Leftists was making fools of the biggest capitalist war machine in the world. The Americans were becoming desperate dropping a greater tonnage of bombs on Hanoi and surrounding areas than the allies dropped in the whole of the World War 2. The 'people' simply and quite literally went underground. They U.S. were randomly using napalm on non-combatants. My father, however, who had voted for the Wilson Labour Government of 1964 thought the British should send troops to help prevent the 'communist domino effect' as it was being called. He had moved Rightwards rapidly. Here are three quotes from Mao's 'Little Red Book' that inspired me and two generations of young people. Not many as young as me though in the West, but I was by no means unique. The world was on fire and the flames were Red and Communist. Here are the three quotes. Mao on the world situation at the time:

People of the world unite and defeat the U.S. aggressors

and their running dogs. People of the world, be courageous,

dare to fight... The whole world will belong to the people.

Chairman Mao on Art and Literature:

Letting a hundred flowers blossom and a hundred

schools of thought contend that is the policy for

promoting the progress of the arts.

Mao on studying:

Complacency is the enemy of study. We cannot really

do anything well until we rid ourselves of complacency.

Our attitude towards ourselves should be 'Insatiable

in studying' and towards others 'Insatiable in teaching.'

Millions of these *Little Red Books* were published by the Foreign Languages Press as were more detailed and specialist collections of Mao: *On Art and Literature* and *Four Essays on Philosophy* and the *Selected Works in Four Volumes* all for next to nothing in price for the student/comrade/*worker*. It is difficult for people now to understand, but millions of people believed as the Black Panther leader, Bobby Seale, who was influenced by Maoism, that the moment had come: '*To Seize the Time.*' We believed the revolution was just around the corner or for some actually present. Young people everywhere were denouncing their professors, teachers, social workers as 'agents of the Yankee capitalist war machine' and as 'reactionaries', 'pigs' and 'running dogs of imperialism', indeed one's parents were seen in much the same way as 'agents of bourgeois social control.' I carried my 'Little Red Book' to school in my blazer book around the age of ten. The other children couldn't comprehend it. We were quite young and they asked me 'if it was my bible.' I replied 'that missed the whole point of Marxist-Leninist thought.' One day at 'Assembly' I stood up at about age eleven and 'denounced' the headmaster as:

'A running dog of Yankee imperialism and lackey of international capitalism.'

No one understood what was happening. I was intellectually advanced, but a child becoming quite disorientated. Indeed a child who was becoming ill. There was the 'counter-culture' and the 'revolutionary Left' and at this time 1966/7-1975 they overlapped., almost cross-pollinated, but also with very genuine disagreements. All these debates: Left versus Right, counterculture versus Revolution, counterculture against Mainstream would contend for hegemony in our family and were magnified and distorted because of the underlying problems delineated in this memoir. Perhaps this was the passage that riveted itself into my mind as the thunderstorms approached:

It is good when we are attacked by the enemy, since it proves

that we have drawn a clear line of demarcation between the

enemy and ourselves. It is better still if the enemy attacks us

And paints us utterly black and without a single virtue; it

demonstrates that we have not only drawn a clear line of

demarcation between the enemy and ourselves, but

achieved a great deal in our work.

- Chairman Mao Tse-Tung.

These would be the lines that Ulrike Meinhoff quoted at the beginning of her theoretical document for the West German Maoist urban guerrilla group the Red Army Faction called *The Urban Guerrilla Concept.* I would later meet R.A.F sympathizers or 'fellow-travellers' at an international youth commune in Birmingham.

They were articulate and knowledgeable in many fields, including European literature and 20th Century European classical music. They took me to Birmingham Town Hall to listen to the City of Birmingham Symphony Orchestra. We would drink and smoke hashish, debating endlessly. For as William Wordsworth, the great English poet, wrote in the 1809 version of *The Prelude* when he supported the French Revolution:

Oh! pleasant exercise of hope and joy!
For mighty were the auxiliars which then stood
Upon our side, we who were strong in love!
Bliss was it in that dawn to be alive,
But to be young was very heaven!—Oh! times,
In which the meagre, stale, forbidding ways
Of custom, law, and statute, took at once
The attraction of a country in romance!
When Reason seemed the most to assert her rights,
When most intent on making of herself
A prime Enchantress—to assist the work
Which then was going forward in her name!
Not favoured spots alone, but the whole earth,
The beauty wore of promise, that which sets
(As at some moment might not be unfelt
Among the bowers of paradise itself )
The budding rose above the rose full blown.

What temper at the prospect did not wake
To happiness unthought of? The inert

# The Flight of Icarus

Were roused, and lively natures rapt away!
They who had fed their childhood upon dreams,
The playfellows of fancy, who had made
All powers of swiftness, subtilty, and strength
Their ministers,—who in lordly wise had stirred
Among the grandest objects of the sense,
And dealt with whatsoever they found there
As if they had within some lurking right
To wield it;—they, too, who, of gentle mood,
Had watched all gentle motions, and to these
Had fitted their own thoughts, schemers more wild,
And in the region of their peaceful selves;—
Now was it that both found, the meek and lofty
Did both find, helpers to their heart's desire,
And stuff at hand, plastic as they could wish;
Were called upon to exercise their skill,
Not in Utopia, subterranean fields,
Or some secreted island, Heaven knows where!
But in the very world, which is the world
Of all of us,—the place where in the end
We find our happiness, or not at all!

Stimulated and engaged I was, indeed, but also tormented by my illnesses. I stayed at The Settlement for a while, but could not avoid readmission to a psychiatric hospital.

But, I travel forward in Time; back in 1967 my sister had started to neglect her appearance because of the drugs and was becoming a hippie. In 1967 she brought home the Donovan double album *A Gift from a Flower to a Garden* in a nice purple box set. When dad found out about the L.P there was a confrontation. Well, he turned on her and she dashed up the stairs to her room. Both were angry, she, because of her personality disorder, not diagnosed at that time and other problems, and he well, who really knows? There was a bitter exchange of words with some quite frankly irrational things said on both sides. He started swinging his fists at her, but she dodged around the bed avoiding them. Then she ran down the stairs and was away. She was found a week later sleeping rough on the beach at Brighten. Of course, there were consequences, she was assigned a social worker. Miss Mac' and he played his usual act of the downcast and wronged father. Hornchurch Social Services were deceived for quite a while, but then Miss Mac' wanted to do a 'home visit' with all the family present at the same time. He got a whiff of trouble ahead and telephoned Social Services and claimed the young woman social worker had 'made a lesbian advance' which as far as I know was utter rubbish. The social worker was taken off the case. However, my sister had been networking at the time with other hippies and drug users. She left again, but this time it was organized and she went to live in a commune in Notting Hill Gate, which was the British version of Height-Ashbury in San Francisco at that time and was the destination for many young runaways. It was ideologically connected to part of Ladbroke Grove, where there were other communes, ideological squats essentially. She used to go down to the Piccadilly Circus, Gerrard Street 'scene' to 'score' opioids. There were not freely available and were restricted to smallish groups of people until the 1980's when Western Europe became swamped by 'brown' heroin from the Middle East. In the late 1960's and 1970's, most, but not all illicit heroin came from the Golden Triangle in the Far East and was a white powder. Luck was not on her side as her 16th birthday would have been on Boxing Day and as the law stood then the authorities couldn't touch her as a 'missing minor'. She was pulled by the plain clothes on Christmas Eve down 'the Dilly', Piccadilly Circus. The opioid users used to inject in the toilets there if they couldn't wait or there was no alternative, but many overdosed. She spent Christmas in a Remand Centre and was then detained in a home for emotionally disturbed girls with high I.Q's at Staines until her eighteeth birthday. As dad was working as a nurse at Fords Dagenham I was taken to Duncroft every other Sunday. The girls there seemed okay to me and they listened as I explained what I was reading at the time. Mum by this time had got me a ticket to the adult library so I could read more advanced books than the material available in the children's section. My sister had come to call the family home 'the fear pit' some time before and the seductions of the Summer of Love were always going to be tempting.

I had been sent to an experimental or progressive school on mum's insistence with the emphasis on creativity, but it wasn't that 'progressive.' Mum had told me:

' Not to write anything about what happens at home in your

stories or the social workers will come and take you away.'

Home just became worse  as time went on the weekends or work holidays being the worst when they had to spend protracted periods together, the arguments and fights. Mum would give me a running commentary about how she was going to put an advertisement in *The Lady* magazine as a gentlewoman's travelling companion and leave. He was working twelve weeks 'days' and then 'nights' and they constantly, mum told me, changed their banking arrangements as a prelude to divorce. Then the Anglican minister Reverent Burg intervened. I don't how he found out other than there were two kind teachers who worked at my school named Mr and Mrs. Booth who went to his church. The Rev. Burg offered them 'Marriage Guidance Counselling' and took me into the choir and one or two of the boys accepted me. Then dad applied for another job and so we moved away.

## A Second Beginning.

A non – writing writer is a monster courting insanity.

**- Franz Kaka.**

In my writing I am acting as a map maker, an explorer
of psychic areas, a cosmonaut of inner space, and I see
no point in exploring areas that have already been
thoroughly surveyed.

**- William S. Burroughs**

L/Spa beckoned like a ballistic missile from another world. The arguments did not abate and I then made the Maoist denouncement of my headmaster, someone should have realized this was not normal behaviour. However, they were different times with different values and there was one boy, Ed, in the sixth form who also read. I think the teaching  staff saw me as a problem to be managed as opposed to a child in need. My parents wanted to send me to a private school, Princethorpe College, its academic standards were high, but I was a Maoist then and so refused to go as a principled stand. Some time later it became apparent what had happened. My English and the most excellent teacher had written to my parents. When I refused to go she tried to get me into a better school. She had petitioned the headmaster, yes the one I had denounced in assembly and said:

'Nigel is like a rose in a desert, he needs

stimulation to grow. If he stays here he

will wilt and die,'

That Patriarchal thug who seemed to think he had been sent by the spectre of Mathew Arnold to keep his pupils in order was frightened of the coming revolution as others were ebullient about a new world in which the bonds of alienation and material need would be abolished and creativity lie at the heart of the human endeavour.

Mum would now disengage with me and my ideological contestation with dad was becoming almost unbearable. My father would vote Tory for the rest of life which was quite a transformation from being a member of the Communist Party of Great Britain, 1934-1937. The house became something to be dreaded and avoided if and when possible. I investigated the C.P.G.P but their 'programme' seemed a betrayal of the Marx, Engels and Lenin I had read. No more than a Leftist version of the Left of the Labour Party. Here was a less than inspiring quote,

> It is the only programme which shows the path
> to Socialism in Britain, taking into account the special
> conditions, traditions and institutions of Britain and the
> utilisation of the democratic gains won by the people
> in years of struggle.

Communist Party of Great Britain, *The British Road to Socialism.*

Both Marx and Lenin were Proletarian Internationalists I had quickly realized who thought the bourgeoisie state must be overthrown. To quote Lenin, which I often did:

> the working class must break up, smash the "ready-made
> state machinery," and not confine itself merely to laying hold
> of it.

Lenin, *State and Revolution.*

I was looking like many of my generation for qualitative dialectical societal transformation and fairly soon. Also, I became beguiled with the poetry of Dylan Thomas, *In my Craft or Sullen Art* was a special favourite, it still is as it encapsulates my *poetic,* indeed an *aesthetic*:

**In My Craft or Sullen Art by Dylan Thomas**

In my craft or sullen art

Exercised in the still night

When only the moon rages

And the lovers lie abed

With all their griefs in their arms,

I labour by singing light

Not for ambition or bread

Or the strut and trade of charms

On the ivory stages

But for the common wages

Of their most secret heart.

Not for the proud man apart

From the raging moon I write

On these spindrift pages

Nor for the towering dead

With their nightingales and psalms

But for the lovers, their arms

Round the griefs of the ages,

Who pay no praise or wages

Nor heed my craft or art.

Then two turns of Fate, I met two 16 year old girls who introduced to many things, including the counterculture scene which rotated around a rundown pub in what was

Satchwell Street called *The Palace.* The back bar consisted of 'Freaks', the front bar of the more criminal working class elements. An anecdote about that pub follows:

'At the age of just before twelve I was in a state of altered

consciousness and accidentally wandered into the front bar,

Big John, a director of less than totally reputable films, picked me

up and deposited me in the back bar. That had been a narrow miss.'

There was a woman of about 20, she had no name and just cruised around the 'scene' with long brown hair and a fur coat. She sniffed cocaine and seemed like an Aphrodite to me. I don't think she had 'relationships' with men or women in carnal or really any other real sense of the word. These people intrigued me. Here was art as life. Or so I thought and would until I sought help with my substance misuse problems at the age of 25. This was not continuous, but intermittent with me and I roamed between various sub-cultures at different times. The girls introduced me to L.S.D., it was beautiful. I saw the purple and the lime- green life energy move through the grass impregnate a tree, dripping-off in golden globules and penetrating my body and mind until I was One with Creation, a hallucinogenic Pantheism and a very vivid experience of Lysergic acid diethylamide  or L.S.D-25. I took to it like Dante to his manuscript. The two teenagers, one of which was would continue her consistent drug use and then grow sympathetic to her Irish Republican roots moving back to the Republic in mid-life. The other girl was so shocked when I choose to take some drugs rather than accept an offer of erotic contact with her; she dropped out of the 'outsider' cultures and back into the mainstream. I have fond memories of them both, there were nice girls, especially 'M'. Not all the teenage Venuses on 'the scene' were quite so pleasant. There was one who seemed to take a pride in out-drugging everyone, female or male. Another who was made pregnant by an older 'cat' always gave me grief. Although I did admire their ingenuity and courage as they arranged to spring the baby from County Council Care and hit the road to where I never knew, but on the whole they were decent good hippie women. Then I started to meet older 'cats', not much though, my sister's generation. I wasn't so keen on these people, but as every drug user knows you have to maintain one's sources, a constant supply. One or two were protective, but most were just pleased to welcome another person into their world. We even used different language to 'the straights' and set ourselves apart from them. Even those of below average intelligence could be taught much under the influence of mind altering drugs. However, soon I was meeting some clever people, both on the chemical drug scene and at the local university. These two currents were separate, even at this time, but as I said previously certainly there was until the mid-1970's some cross-pollination. This occurred once again in the mid-80's. But once I learned the underlying reasons for my substance misuse in therapy and Rehab I then rejected it. Also the counterculture dream was over descended into mass heroin addiction without any 'alternative ideology' and petty-bourgeois commercialism. I could now make a choice: 'I just said No.' But once the doors of perception have been opened by mind-bending drugs it can be difficult to close them again. The discipline of academia and serious writing was my salvation, but I leap ahead of myself rather. Back to the early 1970's. The peculiar thing is that I very rarely bought drugs. People just 'laid-them-on-me'. I think they knew I was ill and thought this was the best solution.

**'Neither Moscow nor Washington but International Socialism.'**

This was the slogan of a large, by far the most substantial Trotskyist current in England known as 'the Party'. They were Neo-Trotskyists. I was to meet a group of their students who were on the local university campus and a light of the organisation teaching at that University. There was also a group of Orthodox Trotskyists affectionately known as the MIG.s [they were the International Marxist Group and MIG fighter-bombers were a key part of the Soviet Union's air force] because there were 'soft' on the defence of what they regarded as a 'degenerated workers state', the U.S.S.R from Imperialist attack. The I.M.G. was in Mandel's 4th International which saw itself as inheriting the mantle of Trotsky's original 4th International. Perhaps its most public figure in the late 1960's-early 1970's was Tariq Ali, who on the attempted storming by a variety of groups of the U.S. Embassy in London protesting the Vietnam War argued in the street, quoting Lenin, 'All power to the soviets' [ a Russian name for a workers council].

The leading theoretician of 'The Party' had been 'bureaucratically excluded' from the Fourth International in 1953 largely because of his line that had developed Trotsky's position on 'the degenerated nature of the U.S.S.R' into a new socioeconomic formulation called 'State Capitalism', he also developed Trotsky's theory of 'Permanent Revolution' into 'Deflected Permanent Revolution' and with Mike Kidron, who left 'The Party', 'the theory of the permanent arms economy.' to explain why they had been a long-post WW 11 boom rather than the world revolution Trotsky expected in 1938-40 to occur after the world war. They saw this 'turn' as a return to the 'Orthodox Marxist' methodology while the I.M.G hung on Trotsky's every word. They were stronger in the universities or 'Red Bases' as they were known from

44

which the revolution would apparently be launched. The Unorthodox Trotskyists had a deeper penetration into the proletariat, but with quite a large student contingent.

I met a 'Party' PhD working at the university teaching Marx and Hegel, who was also a leading member of the organization and some of his students. On a Saturday morning I went to the student's house to discuss theory and Sunday afternoons the lecturer's for the same purpose. I didn't, at that time, have any contact with the working class comrades. I never really did in any meaningful way and when I did my inability to apply theory to the everyday problems of, for instance working at the Fords Foundry in L/Spa was obvious. Yes, as Fate would have it the 'Party' had a 'Factory Cell' where my father was based now as second top nursing officer in the country. This hugely exacerbated the situation at home, but I was now losing control, I was out-of-control. The PhD saw everything as an abstract exercise and he was therefore unaware of my emotional needs. Two of the students quickly realized there was something very wrong, but because of their ideology didn't see psychiatric intervention as a solution. Rather, they started providing a little Newcastle Brown Ale on the Saturday mornings, not much, but in my state of mind I took to it. One day there was someone else sitting round the pine-wood table in the kitchen, I did not like him and his name was 'The Slinker'. This was immediately before the girls gave me that first 'hit' of L. S. D, I was about eleven. However, no Party member ever gave me drugs. It began in chemical-practice with the girls and this was my very first-time, my initiation. 'The Slinker' was not in the 'Party' and older than the university students. This is what happened:

> As usual the discussion was very theoretical, Marxist theory. We
> all sat around debating the finer points and my home problems.
> They at that time would have been considered in an ideological

context. The' youth' was perceived as the supra-oppressed. 'The Slinker' rolled a joint and it was passed around, everyone inhaling deeply. The joint was passed, in turn, to me. For all my turmoil I was quite a sensible little boy. So I said 'No thank you' and passed it on. But then I thought about the hell of home I would have to return to and also my sister's involvement in illicit drugs. I said 'Could I have it back please' and smoked it. The manacles on my mind were thrown off and I left a happy boy. I walked back to the village where my parents lived. Father was downstairs watching ITN World of Sport and mum was upstairs doing the housework. I said to her: 'Mum, I can really understand all the problems you have with dad.' She replied: 'Keep your voice down or we will be for it. She said: 'Have you been taking drugs.' 'Yes', I replied.

She didn't tell anyone, another opportunity for help was missed.

### On the 'Scene.'

I began to steal dad's Nitrazepam and, as he did every night, I mixed them with alcohol. The effect was the same wobble and flop physically and oblivion psychologically. C', one of the university students was alarmed and said if I continued they would have to prevent me from visiting them. It was becoming an Autumn and the people I had regarded as friends were blown away by the gales which would blow me into the gutter, and the children's 'Care' system and then then psychiatric hospitals in quick succession, but I did not lose sight of the stars which are brighter the darker the night. The night was becoming so dark and interminable barren and I knew from my sister, there was an instant galaxy of celestial material which was available through a set of 'works' [syringe]. I decided to confide in her with regard the 'Acid' [L.S.D] and she said to me on the phone:

'I couldn't wait until you were old enough to do your first trip.'

The labyrinth door slammed shut and I went on a 'death-trip' age twelve. I started telling those on the 'scene' who would accept me:

'I am J.J the junior junkie and I won't make 16.'

Many of them did not approve of my politics, but one companion on the descent into Hades is as good as another they seemed to believe. There were some very bright, intellectually, people involved and although they were not 'politicos' in the sense I was they were profoundly interested in literature, philosophy, spirituality and chemistry. They believed that Capitalism was inherently wicked and that a Utopian Commune of people could live within its structures, gradually burrowing away and causing its demise. They did not see the proletariat as the agent of social transformation as Marxists did. Rather, they saw them and the rest of society generally as obedient lemmings obeying orders from an anonymous authority. This 'authority' blighted the lemmings' lives and would ultimately destroy them by overwork and war. It was essentially a fusion of Lifestyle Anarchist ideas with some from the Situationalist International and an awful lot of drugs coming to fruition through the needle of a syringe. As opposed to Mao's concept of revolutionary war achieving victory 'through the barrel of a gun.'

We were under the misapprehension that hallucinogens, stimulants and opioids enhanced creative and intellectual capacity. This was not unusual at the time with role-models like Jean-Paul Sartre using Mescaline to enhance the imagery in *Nausea*, an important 20th century novel and Sartre used amphetamines on a regular basis too:

'Light up the ideas in my mind.'

And of course the residue of 'Beat' culture still existed in the poetry of Diana di Prima, *Allen Ginsberg* and the prose of William Burroughs, Jack Kerouac and Joyce Johnson as well as the recently rediscovered poetry of Elise Cowen. She jumped through a closed seventh floor window pane when her parent's discharged her from mental hospital against doctor's advice. Later they attempted to obliterate her poetry, they burnt it. Fortunately, Leo Skir and others on the 'Beat' scene had some copies and a first complete notebook was published in 2014. Although her work was leaking our little by little, in the magazines and anthologies She is now regarded by literary critics as a major 'Beat' poet, but was destroyed by madness and hard-drugs.

I had seen genuinely pathetic people scribing on long amphetamine binges and becoming psychotic and who have shown me copious pages of random pen marks and saying 'This is really art, man. You know what I mean.' I fell under not quite so profound an illusion about my writing. Not that it was 'great', but the drug facilitated and enhanced it, this is rubbish. I carried out experiments about 1985. With the same list of metaphors and similes I compose two poems: one under the influence of illicit chemicals and one not. The one written **BEFORE** I went 'up' was similar to the poem I composed 'up', but it was more coherent and better constructed technically. This was another reason to seek help, the drugs weren't working creatively. I was beginning to move against the Beat literary aphorism of drug enhanced 'spontaneity' described by Jack Kerouac as' First thought, first word.' We now have, for example, the original 'workings' of Allen Ginsberg's *Howl and* he had revised and 'worked' systematically on it:

### Howl BY ALLEN GINSBERG.

*For Carl Solomon*

I saw the best minds of my generation destroyed by madness,

starving hysterical naked,

dragging themselves through the negro streets at dawn looking

for an angry fix,

angelheaded hipsters burning for the ancient heavenly

connection to the starry dynamo in the machinery of night,

who poverty and tatters and hollow-eyed and high sat up smoking

in the supernatural darkness of cold-water flats floating

across the tops of cities contemplating jazz,

who bared their brains to Heaven under the El and saw

Mohammedan angels staggering on tenement roofs

illuminated,

who passed through universities with radiant cool eyes

hallucinating Arkansas and Blake-light tragedy among the....

But I was moving towards Sylvia Plath's *aesthetic* after reading *Ariel and The Bell Jar.*

I think my poems immediately come out of the sensuous and emotional experiences I have, **but I must say I cannot sympathise with these cries from the heart that are informed by nothing except a needle or a knife, or whatever it is**. I believe that one should be able to control and manipulate experiences, even the most terrific, like madness, being tortured, this sort of experience and one should be able to manipulate these experiences with an informed and an intelligent mind. I think that personal experience is very important, but certainly it shouldn't be a kind of shut-box and mirror looking, narcissistic experience I believe it should be relevant and relevant to the larger things, the bigger things such as Hiroshima and Dachau and so on.

- Sylvia Plath [shortly before her suicide].

So, I had to 'cleanup' and with intensive therapy in the community and also going into a residential Rehab'. Years of struggle, but with support and both studying at the Open University where I gained two Degrees both 2:1's, two Diplomas of Higher Education and I am hoping to begin their Creative Writing M.A this autumn. Also writing for and being published by Chipmunkapublishing, this would be my eighth book. I have no desire to take illicit drugs or drink alcohol. The illnesses remain and the years between twelve and twenty-five I searched for the keys to my enigmas.

## London Calling.

London, the avant-garde counter-culture areas which had welcomed my sister beckoned. I just couldn't remain at home as dad was becoming so angry I was afraid for myself, my life. I had met someone in the counterculture who knew of a far-Left, not 'Party', a commune in Elgin Place just off the Portobello Road. My sister had lived in a hippie squat, but as I have mentioned the ideological divisions between the far-Left, or elements within it, and those seeking Utopian lifestyle choices were not as pronounced in the late 1960's/early 1970's as they would become with essentially these two movements going their own ways.

I met this person in L/Spa as a fluke of being both on the Left and the counter-culture who knew about the commune in Notting Hill Gate. By this time I was 'underground' in Leamington Spa and the streets of this apparently gentile town were paved with amphetamine and L.S.D-25. During the seventies L/Spa became a bit of a counterculture hub itself with small pockets of opioid users as well as the spectrum of other chemicals. This was explained by the hippies because apparently Leamington lies at a crossing of lay lines, but the proximity of motorways and direct access to speed and acid laboratories in Wales probably had more to do with it. Anyway, there was 'fear and loathing' in Leamington Spa' to mimic the title of Hunter. S. Thomson's book about drugs, America and the Sixties. The person I met had concluded that as I couldn't remain at the parental home, staying 'underground' in Leamington as a 'missing minor' was just too risky. So as he knew a person in the Elgin Place squat it would be arranged for me to go to live there. Although, I had to hitchhike down the M1 from near Warwick University and make my own way there. Anyway, I got 'good' lifts and one very bad one from a predatory homosexual paedophile. I managed to escape when he parked the car in some rundown garages in North London. All I will say is 'thank goodness cars didn't come with central locking then!'

I eventually reached my destination, the ideological squat i.e. the commune. My contact there seemed okay and was very well educated so we often talked about books and ideas as we smoked hashish or sampled other drugs and their 'apparent' delights. There was one man in the commune who really disliked me. He had an old 'Royal' typewriter, it was similar to my mum's but he just didn't stop typing for weeks, it turned out to be 'coke' [cocaine] which he was not sharing with everyone else. A sort of Kantian Categorical Imperative at this time amongst drug users was you 'shared your 'gear', your drugs. One day he said to me:

'When it comes to revolutionary theory you are good,

but your practice is not.'

I couldn't decipher exactly what he meant. There were some fairly extreme things happening or planned to happen in the capital at that time. I was a child of thirteen and felt rather vulnerable. Then Guildford, Aldershot and the Old Bailey bombings and the police go berserk. It is 1973, so the Prevention of Terrorism Act 1974 was not on the statute book; it gave the police sweeping powers. So our front door is smashed down at around 5.00 am. One of the older people asks to see the warrant. It was actually sworn out for 'stolen jewellery'. That was absurd. They smashed-up the place after not finding what they were looking for, which appeared to be munitions, it was madness. I was only thirteen. I said that I was seventeen though. But I had to be moved, they may 'sus' I was underage. So by nine that morning I was in a Children of God commune and that was weird. Later I found out that the nicest of them, a young woman, made a call to Social Services and I was picked-up. By this time quite ill.

The social workers took me back to Leamington and said I could go back home. I replied:

'I would rather live in institutions than live there.'

Mum and dad then, without any resistance from mum I must say and with dad saying:

'We can't just sign our child away.'

So I was placed on a voluntary or Section One order under the Children and Young Persons Act, 1969 and taken to Myton Park Assessment Centre. The staff' the childcare officers and the superintendent S.S. [Yes, they really were his initials] had major problems with disturbed drug users of a revolutionary persuasion. However, we also had House Parents, older people and I was lucky in that mine at least tried to understand. They were lovely people, P'&N' but in the end they were out of their depth and said 'we don't understand your behaviour' which was becoming more idiosyncratic as my decline continued.

Then the PhD and his wife, I mentioned previously arranged to 'foster' me, not adoption so I keep my family name, although my biological parents were not *in loco parentis* the local were as they had signed their rights away earlier. This could have worked, but no school would take me because of my 'history' and ideological proclivities although I was still just thirteen. Then I started to gravitate back to the 'scene', who else would accept me? It was a disaster and I went back to London, a rough-sleeper after my brother-in-law turned me away.

**Windsor Park 'People's Free 'Festival' (1974).**

### 1. The Facts.

The first Festival in 1972 was promoted as "Rent Strike: The People's Free Festival", reflecting the political concerns of the organisers (coming as they did from squatting and commune movements), with an anti-monarchist choice of site in "the Queen's back garden". Attendance was about 700 in its first year, rising to 8000 in 1973, and an even larger crowd in its final year. The 1974 Festival, due to last for ten days, was broken up on the sixth morning by a large number of police. Early, on August 29th, 1974 he Festival itself was invaded by hundreds of officers from the Thames Valley police force with truncheons drawn, who gave the remaining participants ten minutes to leave. Those who were arrested or evicted with a level of force that led seven national newspapers to call for an enquiry, and Roy Jenkins, the Home Secretary, to call for a report from the Thames Valley Chief Constable. Nicholas Albery, playwright Heathcote Williams and his partner Diana Senior successfully sued David Holdsworth, the Thames Valley Chief Constable for creating a riotous situation in which the police attacked the plaintiffs.

### 2. The Context.

The year previously the police had killed an I.M.G student from Warwick University during an anti-fascist counter-demonstration in Red Lion Square. That was the first time I had witnessed the 'police protecting the fascists' with quite such force. They just rode into the MIGs on horseback and with truncheons I was twelve.

The Flight of Icarus

### 3. The Experience.

I had hitched down to the 'Free Festival' in Windsor Park. I meet some leftist counterculture friends there. The experiences which I shall delineate were both formative and as I recollect them. It seems like a couple of years ago because of vividness and extremity of it all.

The Park was just covered with hippies and scaffolding on which the stages for the bands were erected. There were Hell's Angels as well; not just bikers, but the real thin with the most wonderful 'chopped' Triumph and Norton motor bikes. There were no police and people were just circulating giving L.S.D away, not asking for a cash-transaction. There were young children who had grown-up in communes and a little friction between the Angels who were 'shooting' pure amphetamine sulphate:

'Man, my tubes are steel man, made of steel yea.'

One of them said to me.

The problem was that they would then get on their bikes and ride around Windsor Great Park and there were little children running about. The dangers were self-evident and eventually, after negotiations an agreement was made to keep them from riding their bikes under the influence of 'speed'. All kinds of hippies were there, I met one man he couldn't have been much more that his late twenties, at the very most, who hadn't washed in years as he injected barbiturates. His hair was tucked-up under a filthy psychedelic headscarf. He looked about seventy and that was the first time I genuinely 'saw tombstones in someone's eyes'. Everyone called each other 'man' or 'cat'. I had seen people inject intravenously in Leamington, but had not myself. My friend who I took a lot of 'acid' [L.S.D.] and speed [amphetamine] which

55

we sniffed using five pound notes was a few years older than me. She would later try and get 'clean, join 'The Party' and attempted a psychology degree at Warwick University. Unfortunately, she didn't have the maths to complete the degree as an awful lot of academic psychology consists of statistical models and she would die young. Far, far too young. We were 'tripped-out' on these green microdots, by this time I had been given the 'name'

'The boy in the green coat, he is far gone man.'

Then towards the end of the festival, before the police stormed it, I had taken a concoction of speed, coke, and acid and I bumped into the barbiturate man who obliged by mainlining, injecting me with some Tuinal. Well, the vein, sort of haemorrhaged there was blood everywhere. My friend claimed that was what prevented her from 'mainlining', taking illicit drugs intravenously. Then Gong was playing on the main stage, it just blew my mind, an astonishing light show, which with the music and drugs stimulated a multi-dimensional almost spiritual experience. Of course I had not slept for ages and was still 'up', but 'coming down'. I came upon a small network of people living under plastic sheeting about three feet of the ground. They didn't stand-up. A voice said' are you the boy I the green coat', someone had gathered me this old relic from the Summer of Love or thereabouts. Yes man'. 'Come in we have something for you.' I gained admission and burrowed in. It was like Coleridge's 'Pleasure Dome' from his poem 'Kublai Kuhn', itself written in laudanum induced reverie. 'I was given a 'hit' of morphine. In a phrase it was one of the most wonderful experiences of mine. It lights up suns in my mind and my body just blossomed. In therapy I would learn 'that I was trying to replicate this experience intermittently for the next twelve years.' It was quite simply beyond comparison in my experience. My sister had made me a hippy shoulder-bag and 'The Man' gave me a set of 'works' in the form of a 'Rocket Syringe' which fitted into a Golden Virginia Tobacco tin, some 'spikes' [needles] and a stock of Omnopon all 'laid on'. The rest of the festival was spent in another dimension all together, a blissful one as there was no problem with building a tolerance too quickly and I had an abundant supply.

#### 4. The Police storming of the festival.

Finally the accumulation of opiates ushered in a deep sleep. The police was known on both the Far-Left and in the Counterculture at that time simply as 'the pigs'. I got the impression the feeling that for the majority of them the feeling was more than amply reciprocated. Anyway, in the early morning I am lying on the grass, essentially in an opiate induced stupor and this boot thumps into my ribs, coming around there were police everywhere, people screaming in terror. The two who has roused me were 'plain clothes', one look said 'drug-squad' to me.

'Ok, get up slowly and open that bag [my shoulder-bag].

One word came into my head 'bust' which was the

counterculture term for arrested in possession of Controlled

Drugs.' Shit Caterogy A and I thought I was thirteen,

a 'missing minor' on the run and on a 'care-order as well.'

They looked at me:

'How old are you.'

'Seventeen'

'Oh yeah. You had better get out of here before the

trouble really starts.'

I had been given a chance, but what choice did you really have. The Hell's Angels put up the stoutest resistance, still high on amphetamine and swinging from the scaffolding and kicking off the police as they tried to storm the stages the bands had been playing on. Then a bit of luck, a Volkswagen Van crammed with hippies picks me up and I am away. They had made a hashish pipe in the back of the van to fortify all. We had escaped. The world was becoming pervaded with significance, everything had gained multi-dimensional significances for me. It was self-evident to most people that I was ill except for the authorities of whatever nature, family, childcare officers, the police, trendy Laingian social workers, the lot. Because I was relatively articulate about bookish or erudite matters people presumed I wasn't ill. This in itself was a form of madness... And as Jim Morrison pointed out when you are strange people are strange. This van was heading for Goldaming, that is where my sister was sent to preparatory school at the age of seven and when we reached their pad it contained several dubious delights, yes, that is correct I had inadvertantavertly stumbled upon a satellite of the London pad and beatitude scene. There was one place these people wanted and that was out, out of it man. That is oblivion, there was a constant round trip to the Picadilly Circus scene and back. Inevitably, these people were overdosing regularly and sure enough, I woke up in Surrey County Hospital. The nurses caught me and my friend trying to inject barbitutes in the bath. He had told me 'the only reason I don't kill myself is my mother.' The nurses guessed my age and said 'we will give you ten minutes before we call the police.' There was nowhere else to run and I awaited the plain clothes, but didn't expect what they would do to me. It was 'heavy', very 'heavy man.'

**Guildford.**

I was escorted to the police station in Guildford by the plain clothes. 1974 was a different world in South East England if they got a whiff of Marxism, particularly Maoism or the Situationalist International because of certain events and there rather florid imaginations. As I was strip searched by three 'officers', they were Detective Constables or D. C's. They even made me pull my foreskin back. There I stood naked and then one left the room only to enter smiling. It was to become really surreal. There was a police series on BBC Television called *'Softly, Softly'* in which one plain clothes come on hard, then the other 'softly, softly'. Two would assault me, then the third say:

'Now you understand I can make this easier if I choose...'

Each needle mark was noted and a weird comment made. They had found some Maoist literature which had really got them going. They thought I was seventeen, but then noticed some lash marks on my back. I genuinely didn't know how it happened. They started knocking me about and finally punched me in the stomach.

'Alright, alright, I am thirteen, a missing minor and just

ring this number and ask for Inspector S. There should

be a W.P.C [Woman Police Constable] in the room when

I am questioned. It is the law, officer.'

They look at each other with bemused glances and back off. I was finally allowed to put on some clothes when the W.P.C came in. So two plain clothes drive down from the Midlands to pick me up. I was detained *incognito* in another Police Station.

**Police, without numbers to identify them**

It became clear I was in the detention cell at L/Spa police station. It was the first cell on the left as they took you down. They had taken my belt and laces as I was a suicide risk. I was ill, both mentally and now physically as I began to withdraw from the chemicals. Disorientated I pressed the alarm button in the vain hope of seeing a police doctor. An adult further down the row of cells was screaming:

'I am on the Register, on the Register please help.'

He meant the Dangerous Drugs Register and, of course, there was no help and his screams continued until they eventually became sobs. A constable with remarkably large black boots came to my cell and said:

'Push that button one more time and see these boots. You'll

get a kicking.'

I began to vomit, sweat and shiver. 'Cold Turkey' in a police cell age 13. Then a couple or so days later a police doctor does arrive and I am taken to Warwick General Hospital. It was in the evening, the young civilian doctor said you are too young for 'a substitute and it will be over in the next few days. He didn't have to go through it. They back to the Station, what became known as 'The Temple of Darkness' as I slipped into psychosis over the next months.

Then 'withdraw' over. Now came the group from, I presumed from their accents Birmingham. There were no means to identify them. I was taken for 'questioning' into an office. There were five or six of them. One took out a key and locked us in. I thought revolutionaries can die in these circumstances. The questioning was truncated and intermittent and the assaults protracted. Problem was, I explained:

'I can't tell you what I don't know.'

They had some ideas about the Situationist International in Britain: 'The Angry Brigade', and Irish Republican activities, drug dealing networks. Delusional stuff essentially. But after about six or seven hours of this I realized that things could get extremely bleak, to use a euphemism.

'I will admit to having taken proscribed drugs in

a written and signed statement for court. If this

all stops.'

Back to the cells, still in my vomit covered tee shirt and before three magistrates the next morning. No criminal charges were made. at that time there was an underground passage from the police station to the adjacent Magistrates Courts. Three officers, two uniformed and a D.C. escorted me and yes, they roughed me up in the tunnel connecting the two buildings. Mum was sitting at the back of court, but not dad. She was asked if she had anything to say:

'He was such a good boy.'

The magistrates place me on a Section 3 Care Order under the Child and Young Persons Act 1959 until I was eighteen because I was I need of 'care and protection' and in 'moral jeopardy. A magistrate asked me if I had anything to say to which I did not reply. I didn't recognize bourgeois justice, although it had recognized me. The headlines in the local daily, *The Morning News* were '**Junky in 14'.** I wasn't quite 14, but it was close, it had been very close.

**Myton Park Centre the second visit and I meet a forensic psychiatrist.**

You can imagine the Superintendent S.S was just delighted to have me back in his 'care and protection'. I arrived at about 11.00 a.m. The other kids had been funnelled into whatever institution was seen fit from them. Unfortunately, I had left an indelible mark on his right-wing heart, true blue and cold as a death. He had the aura of the great reformer; he certainly did not like recidivist communist hippies, known in the U.S.A. as Yippees briefly. My sister had given me a copy of Jerry Rubin's 'Do It. Scenarios Of The Revolution.' I wasn't that impressed by Rubin's book and he would later capitulate to American Capitalism and become a stockbroker on Wall Street. The other children had also heard of me through some kind of grapevine, which linked all kids-in-care. There was a welcoming present me for me. About an hour I was processed, an anonymous man turned-up, apparently a childcare officer. To cut a convoluted tale short, I ended-up naked in a bath of about three inches of not particular diluted bleach.

'All communists are dirty. All junkies are dirty.'

He said and leered at me. Then I was cleaned-up and he had gone. He had been brought in 'to teach me a lesson' and 'to soften me up.' S.S didn't do politicos. One escaped and lived underground working in a bakery up North until his 'Care Order' had expired. Another was forced to fight with me. We both refused, but the pressure became unbearable and he apologised and struck me. Things were going from night to the void fairly quickly. My non-residential Social Worker was a Marxist, most were in the 1970's. Sort of red moles burrowing into the system. He took me out for 'tea' and showed me the report a psychiatrist who saw me twice for a few minutes and had prescribed some medication had made. It said:

'Pearce should be detained in a disciplined and punitive unit

until at least 18 to correct his deviant ideological proclivities.'

So I was political prisoner and we didn't like the sound of 'at least' i.e. post my 'Care Order' expiring. This old doctor had been known when he visited at Myton Park, with other children, to wipe out a cross, a crucifixion model and hold it front of them muttering. He was weird. The Superintendent S.S could have manipulated him for his own ideological agenda, this was a possibility. So my social worker and mother appealed and asked for a 'second opinion, and I saw a forensic psychiatrist from Winston Green Prison in Birmingham on the Thursday and the next Monday I transferred to the Regional adolescent Unit at Hollymoor Hospital in Northfield, Birmingham. He had said:

'You should be in the system, but you are in the wrong system. You

need to in the psychiatric system.'
Dr. J.H [Forensic Psychiatrist].

Within a couple of weeks I was on Ward 19 or 19s [most of the wards were known by their numbers by both staff and patients. 19s was a locked adult male ward and 5s, a locked female adult ward. There was a girl who was regularly moved to 5s and me who, after this 'move' would in future be sent to 20s, an open adult male ward until 'well' enough to be returned to 'The Unit' as it was known. The girl would go the Brownhills mental hospital after 16 and me first to the Birmingham Settlement, Professor T's experimental unit at the Q.E then to Central Hospital. I asked a consultant about a boy at Myton Park and was told he was 'too ill' to come to 'The Unit'. Once I was told I was 'too ill' to be at that hospital. You learnt that meant indefinitely 'down South' or Moss Side, both were certainly to be avoided.

Nigel Pearce

**Hollymoor Hospital.**

I was a patient here from just before my fourteenth birthday until age 16. It was the first real home, I had. I wasn't 'punished' for being ill. Of course with the 'history' the consultants Drs I' and C' the former the country's leading expert on adolescent psychiatry who worked on 'The Unit' full-time and the latter, a forensic psychiatrist worked part-time were a little weary, but we soon got on quite amicably. Dr. I' was a real 'bluestocking' in the proper sense of the word, a woman who had devoted her life to intellectual pursuits. The latter, who delighted in coming to 'The Unit' and greeting me with a smile after attending either Birmingham Crown Court or a Mental Health Tribunal:

'Two more for Broadmoor and one to Rampton today Nigel. Very satisfying.' He beamed. 'Yes, Dr. C'. I would reply to this or variants on it.

I kept quiet about the 'struggle' while in hospital. This is always a wise move. However, I did meet a very remarkable psychiatrist, a senior registrar, Dr. Helen W' who was crippled with arthritis. She took an interest in me and we would discuss many things. She introduced me to Jungian psychology. The types of medication were I took have had a continuity from those days until today, other than they won't prescribe Valium and Librium for me anymore. 40 years on, this came as a bit of shock to the system. But the rest remains, anti-psychotics, anti-depressants, mood-stabilizers and sleeping tablets. 'The Unit' was in many ways, for me anyway, integrated into the adult hospital. Although it had a school because of the 1944 Education Act, Dr.I' decided I was 'too ill' to attend five days a week and so 'worked' on 'the gardens' two days a week with the adult patients. Yes, the patients did 'work' and were utilized to keep the fairly extensive 'grounds' of the hospital in order. The

64

deputy-head, gardener brewed this thick, strong and sweet churn' of tea on a gas ring in the potting sheds all morning and then at eleven the 'patients' had tea and cheese sandwiches. Huge wads of bread and cheese and as I was the youngest I was given the crust one, a treat. Fuelled we returned to tending the grounds of the asylum which largely entailed raking grass. These places had massive expenses of lawns. He was married to the deputy sister on the adolescent unit. All the staff sort of interbreed, I wondered if after generations of this there would a form of madness engendered, maybe. When 'ill' I would be restrained and given intramuscular injections of Chlorpromazine and 'wake-up' eight or so hours later in bed with two nurses sitting at the foot of my bed, this was known by both patients and staff as being 'specialed'. The nurses went everywhere with you, even the toilet. Then the doctors would decide whether or not to 'go with the flow' or send me to 20's, the adult ward. I was not abused at Hollymoor though in the way I had been at Myton Park.

Every two weeks all the patients went into this huge hall to watch a film. They had a real double-reeled film projector which flickered through the film. The 'kids' were taken into' Northfield' shopping on a Saturday morning and to a film at the cinema at The Odeon on the Bristol Road in the afternoon when well enough, but were closely supervised. There was a number 61 bus from outside the hospital through Northfield, along the Bristol Road, which stopped at Navigation Street in the City Centre, conveniently close to Hudson's Bookshops which were on multiple sites. Most of the staff were okay, some took me out for a drink on occasion. The boys and girls had 'relationships' that the staff condoned and at times with some other matters, well a 'blind eye' was cast. It was the 1970's; the world was a different more relaxed place. The staff had 'trained' during the Summer of Love and in its aftermath.

**Interesting Times at The Birmingham Settlement**

The Birmingham Settlement was an international youth project in Summer Lane, New Town. It took 'carefully selected' boys and girls in-care, students from Aston and Birmingham University, a few young people with jobs and some from West Germany, one from East Germany and several from Holland. The Dutch and German people were on the Left of the Left and in earnest, very intense people, rather like me at that time. They took soft drugs and drunk a lot and we discussed for many a night the Red Army Faction, the Popular Front for the Liberation of Palestine and Action directe (AD) in France. I would a few years later meet a young woman close to (AD) back at L/Spa. Although her ideological credentials were not known by many. She had a mass of long red hair and an inclination towards the consumption of cocaine. All these people returned to Europe.

The children-in-care were also radicalized on the whole, but with the exception of me weren't really accepted by the students and other young people. Two notable exceptions were B.B. and P.D. Both 'jumping' their 'care-orders' and going 'underground' with two of the Dutch women. The 'armed struggle' was on the agenda at that time of the Far Left i.e. beyond the Trotskyist Left who saw it as a distraction from building a mass movement of workers in the trade unions. You just couldn't ignore it. The 'second generation' of the Red Army Faction included members of the Socialist Patients' Collective (in German: Sozialistisches Patientenkollektiv, and known as the SPK) were a psychiatric patients' collective founded in Heidelberg University, Germany. In what was known as the German Autumn of 1977, R.A.F. /S.P.K almost brought the West German State down, at least to its knees.

Also, I had discovered via reading Jung and talking to young Catholics and through protracted discussions with a Roman Catholic priest, Father Liam' at that time Roman Catholicism was in the immediate aftermath of Vatican 2 and the Leftward 'turn' of the church with some attempting a synthesis of Catholicism and Marxism. This 'Liberation Theology' was a dominant form in Latin America with Father Camillo Torres both fighting with Che Guevara and dying on 'active service' with the FARC, the Revolutionary Armed Forces of Colombia. Even in England, where Liberation Theology was marginalised books like Peter Hebblethwaite *The Christian-Marxist Dialogue and Beyond* were read by the Left intelligentsia in the Church.

The problem I had was that not being properly 'grounded' and with a variety of psychiatric disorders, plus the drugs was a little too much. There was Acid [L.S.D] from time to time at the Settlement and a couple of acid casualties obsessed with Leonard Cohen, everyone kept an eye on every Bod Dylan album, but also much classical music was listened to both recorded and at Birmingham Town Hall, at the time the home of the City of Birmingham Symphony Orchestra. Nevertheless, as I was becoming ill, not for the last time well-intentioned, but ill-informed people with a Radical Anti-Psychiatry agenda, just could not accept that 'illness' in the clinical sense existed. I accepted these arguments, but often the State mental health services were left to pick up the pieces. So it was I was found a little disorientated in Coventry with a note asking to take me back to 'The Settlement'. The doctors were not amused, although I took the can. I stayed in touch with a young German woman from The Settlement for several years, but she became convinced that our mail was opened by Special Branch and she was being watched... so we decided it sensible to sever tangible links. Although I will never forget her.

## Professor T's Experiential Unit at the Q.E.

Taken back to 'The Unit' to be 'held' as I was still on the 'care order' and Dr.I phoned Prof T' and asks if he has a bed. He took mainly fairly high functional psychosis and mood-swing, 'manic-depressive psychosis'. Which I was diagnosed at the time. He did, so I have been admitted there just after my sixteenth birthday. He had two wards: one was low stimulation, i.e, no books, music etc and the other high stimulation which are self-evident. He was writing a paper on the consequences of the withdrawal of stimulation to high functioning patients with manic-depressive psychosis. The study was a little academically flawed though, because after the doctors left in the early evening the nurses let us do as we wished and mix freely between both of the 'control groups.'

I had been depressed in a state of semi-catatonia and then had a burst of energy and absconded. I was on 'bed-rest' at the time and ran from the Q.E along the Bristol Road to New Street Station. I had some vague notion of contacting mum, but I was in hospital issue pyjamas. The police spotted me and asked me where I came from. I replied:

'I am from Professor T's experimental manic-depressive unit.'

They said:

'Come on we are taking you back.'

Upon my return the nurses gave me a wallop of intramuscular Chlorpromazine. Then I became an exemplary patient, but was on my way up or possibly normal Nigelness. Anyway, I quietly read Trotsky: *History of the Spanish Revolution* and George Orwell: *Homage to Catalonia*. Prof T' takes into this lecture theatre and sits next to me while medical students are ready to take notes. Anyway, I get into gear and begin explaining the situation in Spain at the time before and during the Civil War from a Trotskyist perspective. I didn't mean any harm, but these students begin to scribble notes accordingly. Prof T' begins to smile and after half an hour is smiling with delight.

'That is quite enough now Nigel. Back to the ward.'

I wasn't given an injection of Largactil but a tot of that horrid brown syrup and then go to sleep. I go back into semi-catatonia. They would not let me use much of the experimental technology on the ward such as 'bio-feedback machines'. Then he said that he would like to 'try E.C.T.', I say 'No, no way.'

Trouble was Social Services were *In Loco Parentis* until I am eighteen and they would not contradict a Professor of Psychiatry. I contact mum how wrote to the local Tory M.P. I was shown the letter years later by a non-residential social worker. The M.P had written:

'I do not find it appropriate to give a minor E.C.T against both

his wishes and those of his parents.'

Back on bed-rest and they brought a mobile E.C.T machine to my bed. Two weeks, four shocks, no choice. Later, at Central Hospital they gave me 12 more blasts of electricity. Everyone on the admission wards had it for a period at Central, it didn't matter what the diagnosis was on Tuesdays and Fridays. After you came round in the 'recovery room', a treat of a cup of tea and digestive biscuits. Quite frankly, you wouldn't know where you were for a day or so afterwards, it was grim, we were mainly young people. But there were 'Red' staff how tried to ameliorate matters.

**'Pearce, he is a real no hoper.'**

As the sister handed over to the night staff, she described me as:

'That is a real no hoper.'

I knew, though the philosophy and literature I was reading, she would properly struggle with. This is one of the reasons my relationships with most doctors was better than the nurses. They had done the reading; of course, there were a notable exception to this generalization on both sides. This is inherent in the nature, making broad brush stroke statements. Dr Joyce and I would talk for hours about books, the nature of fulfilment and she continued an interest in Jungian psychology began at 'The Unit' by Dr. Helen. Other examples where the French Matron at Central Hospital, which had around 800 patients. Although not many of them were floridly ill. Rene and I would sit on a bench in the grounds in intense and rewarding conversation about French Existentialism in all its manifestations. She had been to lectures at The Sorbonne taught by Simone de Beauvoir. There was a night sister, the mother of a present day psychologist. She knew an awful lot about poetry, and many nights we would stay up 'talking poetry.' Also acts of kindness by a Spanish night's Nursing Assistant who always brought a mug of milk and a sandwich. His family had fled fascism in Spain; they had been on the losing side at the end of the Spanish Civil War, where my father's friend and comrade had fought with the International Brigades. Another puffed-up little nurse said:

'You are not as intelligent as you think you are.'

Dr. Joyce, my consultant, tore him to shreds and he never repeated the experiences

70

The Flight of Icarus

So, I had my supporters and my detractors amongst the staff. One rather vicious Charge-Nurse gave me an injection of Largactil P.R.N and while other nurses held me in place rammed the needle into its plastic base and he said:

'You will remember that.'

I do remember him and the incident well, a little fascist runt. Having said that there were also I.M.G nurses I knew from outside who would make clenched fist salutes, the normal form of mutual recognition between Trotskyists and smuggle volumes of, for example, Trotsky: *On Art and Literature*. There was one of their comrades in there also who became a friend. He played the clarinet beautifully.

Things really did become difficult when there were ill-informed Christian fundamentalists in positions of middle management in the early 1980's. They were biblical literalists who believed the apocalypse was imminent and the U.S.S.R was satanic and that after a nuclear exchange The Second Coming would occur, real religious zealots. The problem was if they had been a nuclear exchange between the West and the U.S.S.R that would have been it, the end,false stop. What scientists at the time called 'The Nuclear Winter.' I had the misfortune to 'cross' one of these Christians on the question of C.N.D [Campaign for Nuclear Disarmament] and stream of invective poured from the lips, Mrs.B ':

'You are wallowing in evil and you are hand in hand with the devil.'

The problem was the nursing officer went to the same Evangelical Church. All of this because of their eccentric belief systems which were on the fringes then, but we have regrettably seen Fundimentalism dominant religious discorse, I find this sad.

71

**The 'Turn' to academia.**

1986 and I was returning the Earth's orbit after a year rotating around the moon and was being nursed by an excellent ward Sister K' and a consultant Doctor C' who both spotted potential. After the experiences delineated in this memoir, which withholds much information, you can imagine I was quite a wreak with little confidence. Sister K' was the driving force with Dr. C overseeing the whole scheme. The cleaning ladies bucket room was turned into a room which became known as Nigel's study, it was locked with a table and chair and study materials from and relating to The Open University. G.M., an inspiring lecturer, visited me in the hospital twice a week for gradually longer and more demanding sessions. Eventually I left the hospital and went to live in a 24 hour staffed pre-discharge unit in the community. Here I worked with less support, but systematically. I would become ill without the stimulus of any illicit drug and on occasion Dr. would enforce a 'no-study period' or admit me to the new hospital. Sometimes I would be advised to take a year 'out.' but this was becoming, with my creative writing, a life-line.

Two years in this unit, then a group home for five years, another uninduced florid episode and Dr. wants to put me in long term residential care. I persuade him to give me a chance in another group home. My drug problems resolved by the Drug Misuse Team, principally J'. Rayner and then into Rehab for the *delirium tremens*. I came to live in my flat in 1999. It is great, books and writing and study materials as well as and music, particularly J. S. Bach the year after I finally graduated when. Dad said

'This is the greatest day of my life.'

Dad had taken an interest in my degree and we were finally reconciled, thank goodness during his life.

**The 'turn' to Chipmunkapublishing.**

This will be my eighth book with Chipmunkapublishing. A nurse named Nancy T' noticed an article about Jason Pegler and his company Chipmunkapublishing. She knew I wrote and had bits and pieces published and gave me the article. This 'turn' which has enhanced my being in the same fashion The Open University did and does. So I now have a second degree B.A. (Hons) Humanities with Creative Writing and hope to start the Creative Writing Masters Programme in the Autumn. This is a consequence of writing for and being published by Chipmunkapublishing and last year I was very pleased to become one of five Chipmunka Classics authors.

**Some musing on aesthetics in writing.**

Bertolt Brecht uses history to reflect upon the present with reference to the play *Life of Galileo*. For my study I use one text in favour of my position on Brecht that he did use History to reflect on the present and one against it to create the tension necessary in dialectical disputation. Boal (2008) *Theatre of the Oppressed* to affirm it and Thomas Mann (1998) *Mass und Vert* as its negation. I located Boal, A (2008) Theatre of the Oppressed, London: Plato Press in Wallis, M, Shepard, S (2013) Studying Plays, London: Bloomsbury which augments my reading and purchased Boal (2008). The relevance of Augustus Boal (2008) to my analysis of Brecht is important for two reasons. Firstly, because he developed the theory of 'Aristotle's Coercive System of Tragedy' then through a Marxist reading of Hegelian aesthetics showed Brechtian drama as its historical opposite. The question of 'form' pervaded aesthetics from Aristotle through Hegel and Marx to the debates between Brecht and Lukacs in the 20th century. Thus, there is a relationship between aesthetic form and History. Boal argues:

> Aristotle's coercive system of tragedy survives to this day,
>
> thanks to its great efficacy. It is in effect a system of intimidation.

Boal (2008) p. 40.

Questions posed by Boal are a) what is the nature of Aristotle's tragic method b) why is it coercive and c) how can it as a hegemonic 'form' be challenged over Time? Boal seeks explanation by revisiting some key concepts:

> In the beginning, the theatre was the chorus, the mass of people.

Ibid p.29.

Theis is creating a protagonist 'aristocratised' drama. A division was created between the masses (Chorus) and aristocracy. The Tragic Hero emerged when the State, who financed the arts, employed the theatre as a means of political domination. At that moment drama becomes a weapon of class struggle.

Boal, then outlines how Aristotle's Poetics function as a method of social control. An Aristotelian tragedy has predetermined structure. An exposition during which empathy is created between the spectators and the characters, not just the Tragic Hero and as the drama proceeds both Ethos and Diana are created. The Ethos is the action and the Dianoia the reasoning for this activity, but as they must each exist to perpetuate the other Boal says just call it Ethos. For Aristotelian drama, in Boal's reading, Ethos contains Virtue and reflects a balanced society and as the Tragic Hero is emblematic of the aristocracy he embodies the 'virtues' of that class. However, *harmatha* must be present in the Tragic Hero; this is a 'tragic fault' or deviation from Ethos. The play reaches its climax; the hero has a moment of realization or *perpeteia* when he realizes he has transgressed society's norms. He takes a fall and is then transformed by *anagnorisis* and a catharsis takes place. Thus societal norms are created, broken and then corrected in accordance with the ruling ideology. The audience who has been 'feeling' this process is then likewise 'purged' of any deviant traits. This is what Boal meant by 'Aristotle's Coercive System of Tragedy'.

Boal argues that Aristotle's formulaic system is successful, but he concludes:

> ...if we want to stimulate the spectator to transform his
>
> society, to engage in revolutionary action, in that case

we have to seek another poetics!

ibid p.42.

He then traces the development of Aristotle through Hegelian aesthetics:

In these two philosophers the drama shows the external

collision of forces originating internally – the objective

conflict of subjective forces. For Brecht everything is

reversed.

Ibid, p 73.

Explained as Aristotle and Hegel's representation of the character – subject relationship and Brecht's character – object relation we see the former as an expression of the inner life of the character and the latter as the expression of external social processes.

Boal concludes Brecht should have called his work 'Marxist poetics' not 'dialectical poetics' (Boal p 78). I agree with his interpretation of Aristotelian - Hegelian aesthetics in History and Brechtian theatre. I endeavour to apply these concepts to my argument regarding the *Life of Galileo*. My second evaluative bibliography is Thomas Mann, Mann, T, *Mass und Vert* in Bentley, E (1999) Bentley on Brecht, New York: Applause, pp. 32-34.I found this article in Thomas Mann's literary journal Mass und Vert (Measure and Value) in Bentley (1999 pp. 32-34) a collection of essays which are cited in Walder, D (2005) Bertolt Brecht, Life of Galileo, Aesthetics and Modernism: texts and debates, Milton Keynes: Routledge and The Open University. The extracts from Mass and Vert and other material cited are not in the course materials. In the preamble Eric Bentley ushered the reader into the literary debate between Bertolt Brecht and Thomas Mann in its historical context:

> To Thomas Mann, who described Brecht as "very
>
> gifted", the whole Brechtian world's distasteful.
>
> Bentley (1999) p. 32.

He notes *Mass and Vert* was a Mann's journal for articulating his poetics. Bentley comments that Mann wrote the article, but he used a pseudonym. Nevertheless, Thomas Mann provides a counterexample to my argument in favour of Brechtian poetics. George Lukacs, another of Brecht's adversaries, this one an Orthodox Marxist, described Thomas Mann as 'the bourgeois behind the bourgeois world' or the creator of 'critical realism' as Lunn (1984, p.83) mentions Mann wrote six theses in his article. I have selected three of them. Firstly, parodying 'art for art's sake', he claims:

> That Brecht's work is "propaganda for propaganda sake".
>
> Bentley, p. 33.

This by implication is suggesting that instrumentalist art is inferior to the material of an aesthete. Something I contest in my argument for two reasons. Firstly, for example, the novels of Maxim Gorky have aesthetic value as well as propaganda potential as Socialist Realism; This is true of any capable writer who puts their pen to didactic employment. Secondly, in highly contested historical epochs like both Seventeenth Century and Twentieth Century published writers may be obliged ethically to write instrumentally because of Kant's 'Categorical Imperative':

Act only according to that maxim whereby you can, at

the same time, will that it should become a universal law.

Kant (1785] 2011) p. 515.

Mann's fourth argument:

His people have no memory. They are the opposite of

Ibsen's characters... They are no cracks through which

the past presses through.

Bentley (1999) p. 33

Mann is not saying Brecht has no historical characters, but they are 'flat' characters. This is incorrect because Galileo is not a 'stock-character', he experiences metamorphosis, he remembers and regrets. He is a theoretician who developed a methodology he later renounced. Mann's sixth thesis is that there is a contradiction between Brecht's claim for objective science and didactics. This is the whole point of 'dialectical theatre' is that it creates a contradiction.

Bentley (1996) is absolutely clear about his position regarding Brecht:

I did not share his politics or the philosophy behind them.

Ibid, p, 13.

The second part of my analysis begins as follows:

The history of all hitherto existing societies is the history of class struggle.

Marx & Engels (1955) p. 34.

My thesis employs material in the evaluative bibliography. However, I address the broader questions of Life of Galileo and Brecht in historical context. I shall argue consistently from a Marxist position, but in that process examine other critiques. The historical narrative of World War 1, and the crisis of Weiner Germany, which became part of a generalized crisis of capitalism caused by the dialectical fault lines within capitalism as well as it twin motors toward economic crisis a) the 'over accumulation of Capital' and b) the 'law of the tendency of the rate of profit to fall', both articulated by Marx. These led to the rise of Fascism, the Stalinist bureaucracy, the world economic recession and World War 11 during the latter American Atomic bombing of Hiroshima killed tens of thousands of people in one day. Brecht was appalled to see the productive forces of humanity unleashed in such a destructive manner. As a Marxist, he would have believed in the productive potential of the science. All of this helped mould the play text and performance history of *Life of Galileo*. Therefore, three versions were written and performed in this period: Zurich (1938), American (1947) and Berlin (1957), the year after Brecht's death. All of which reflected the changing objective material conditions. As Brecht noted in his diaries in 1938:

> Amid the darkness gathering fast over a fevered world,
>
> a world surrounded by bloody deeds and no less bloody
>
> thoughts, by increasing barbarism which seems to be leading
>
> irresistibly to perhaps the greatest and most terrible war of
>
> all time, it is difficult to adopt an attitude appropriate to people
>
> on the threshold of a new and terrible age.

Unwin (2005). p.193

Brecht's theatre is informed by variations on a theme of his Marxist worldview which he held from 1926 when he read Karl Marx Capital. My mission statement is completed by stating that my close reading of Life of Galileo will show that it is analogous and indeed 'reflects' on the present. In conclusion, I argue that Brecht subverted Aristotelian Theatre generally, also the Berlin premiere by his notes on Mao (1937 [1968]) *On Contradiction* and in the milieu of Modernism he leaves a fragmented question unanswered, the Dialectic unresolved.

In *Capital, Marx* employed the methodologies of dialectical materialism and historical materialism to expose the hidden laws of classical capitalist mode of production, particularly the nature of commodity fetishism and the innate tendency of capitalism towards economic crisis, I would argue that these elements were salient in Brecht as a writer living in a declining capitalist society. Marx, describing commodity fetishism illuminated three elements within Modernism: alienation, dehumanization of human relations and fragmentation of society caused by mode of production, decaying capitalism. I quote an extract from the section on commodity fetishism at some length because of its relevance to the question of Brechtian theatre and Modernism in general:

> But it is different with commodities. There, the existence of the
>
> things quâ commodities, and the value relation between the
>
> products of labour which stamps them as commodities, have
>
> absolutely no connection with their physical properties and with
>
> the material relations arising therefrom. There it is a definite social
>
> relation between men, that assumes, in their eyes, the fantastic form

of a relation between things. In order, therefore, to find an analogy,

we must have recourse to the mist-enveloped regions of the religious

world. In that world the productions of the human brain appear as

independent beings endowed with life, and entering into relation both

with one another and the human race. So it is in the world of

commodities with the products of men's hands. This I call the

Fetishism which attaches itself to the products of labour, so soon as

they are produced as commodities, and which is therefore inseparable

from the production of commodities.

Marx ([1867] 1955) Vol 1, pp. 163-4

But for Marx the 'class conscious' worker or intellectual is not a passive 'spectator' on the stage of history, 'The philosophers have only interpreted the world, the point however, is to change it (Marx 2007) p. 172.. I would argue that in Capital and Thesis on Feuerbach quoted above directly informed Brecht's theory and practice.

If the writer is going to act in history, he will need a new poetics according to Boal (2008 p. 42) who I quoted thus in Part 1 'if we want to stimulate the spectator to transform his society, to engage in revolutionary action, in that case we have to seek another poetics!' Brecht did 'create another poetics which Boal argues he located the nexus of Marx's materialist understanding of Hegelian dialectical philosophy and aesthetics. Essentially, it is possible to perceive three phases of Brecht's dramaulogy. The first of Lebhrsuck or 'parade play, but then importantly around the end of the 1920's Brecht become interested in Gustus or 'socially-encoded expression' (Mumford, p. 53) which Brecht (1964) The Theatre of Bertolt Brecht expands upon:

It is at once gesture and gist, attitude and point: one aspect of the

relationship between two people, studied singularly, cut to essentials

and physically or psychologically neutral. It excludes the psychological,

The sub-conscious, the metaphysical, unless they can be conveyed

concrete terms.

Mumford (2009) p 54-55.

An example of Gestus is presented in Life of Galileo , is the recantation scene 13, when in the 1975 film Virginia is on a bare stage apart from Galileo's disciples, saying 'murmured' [stage direction] 'Ava Marias' then bell of St.Marks rings to show he has renounced his scientific beliefs and her only line in the scene is:

'He's not damned.'

Brecht (2013) p.97.

We are 'shown', not 'told' the gulf between the two world systems. For as Jameson (2000) Brecht and Method argued Brecht does not use blunt didactic methods but:

The showing of showing, the showing how you show and

demonstrate.

Keller, p. 60.

However, as this is, as Brecht noted, 'dialectical theatre' and dialectics is a play between thesis and antithesis, a 'unity of opposites' (Engels). Galileo is not damned according to Roman Catholicism, but is with the future of Humanity because he recants the scientific and empirical proof of the Copernican System. There is an allegorical relationship between Galileo's era and what novelist, poet and essayist Victor Serge called in the title of one of his novels 'Midnight in the Century [1939] when the Stalinist bureaucracy were attempting to eliminate the revolutionary tradition which consisted of Trotsky and his group and the other ' Oppositionists'. Scene 13 continues with one of the best known exchanges in Brecht's poetics:

Andrea loudly: Unhappy the land that has no heroes.

...

Galileo: No, unhappy the land where heroes are needed.

Brecht (2013) p. 98.

In the G.D.R in 1957, the year the Berlin version was first performed, this would have had resolutions about the concept of 'the cult of personality' where an, almost, apotheosis occurs to the hero/leader. This was an integral part of the Stalinist tradition, but is inimitable to the Trotskyist.

A counterexample to the cogency of the Brechtian method was contained in my second evaluative bibliography. The theses written by Thomas Mann under a pseudonym in his journal Mass und Vert. In one of these he argues as follows: 'His people have no memory. They are the opposite of Ibsen's characters...They are no cracks through which the past presses through'. Thomas Mann critique is really about 'form'. Are Brecht's characters in the tradition of Classical Realism, clearly not.

But there is an instance in Life of Galileo where he does appear to fall into the Socialist Realist which in-itself would be an anathema to Mann. In *Brecht,* 2013 pp. 107-109 scene 14 Galileo:

> … If the scientists brought to heel by self – interested rulers,
>
> limit themselves to pilling up knowledge for knowledge
>
> sake, then science can be crippled and your new machines
>
> lead to nothing but process way from mankind.

> Brecht (2013) pp. 107-109.

There is however huge irony here because the stage direction (Breght, p.107) reads:

> Galileo professorially, folding is hands over his stomach.

And he has just said to Andrea:

> … Welcome to the gutter, brother in science and cousin in betrayal.

> Ibid, p. 109.

Brecht has just parodied Socialist Realism in its defense of science and the aesthete's ethic in 'knowledge for knowledge's sake' mirrors 'art for art's sake and replies to Mann's 'propaganda for propaganda's sake'. It is also a commentary on that great aesthete Oscar Wilde's 'We are all in the gutter, but some of us are looking at the stars' Lady Windermere's Fan, A Play About a Good Woman (1892), Lord Darlington, Act III. So what is Brecht doing here? By the time he was back in Germany, the G.D.R, he had developed the concept of 'complex seeing' by which Unwin (1988) maintains:

84

> He wanted to make the contradictions visible and show
>
> the causal links between ... money and power and expose
>
> the different sides of the arument in such a way as to
>
> encourage debate.

Unwin (1988) p 55.

The 12 the Grand Inquisitor, he is never given a name but the title, which creates foreboding, and the former Cardinal Barberini a mathematician are in a dialogue about Galileo teachings while the Pope is being robbed. Without his robes Urban VIII has a certain respect for science. However The Grand Inquisitor after a little debate and prevarication gets to the point:

> Who really cares how these spheres rotate, but thanks to this
>
> little wretched Florentine all Italy, down to the lowest stable boy,
>
> is now gossiping about the phases of Venus.

Brecht (2013) p.92.

Of course Galilei's greatest crime was writing in the vernacular. As the Pope's has garment upon garment put on the defamiliarization or 'Alienation Effect' focuses the audience's Reason rather than their emotions about him, here is where Brecht deviates from the Naturalist tradition of Ibsen. Finally the fully robed Urban VIII concedes the error on the Church's authority. Brecht is clearly showing the Church as the ideological voice of the ruling class. He says:

> At the very most he can be shown the instruments.

That will be quite enough your Holiness. Instruments are

Mr. Galilei's specialty.

ibid, p.94.

The audience may see a smirk coming over The Inquisitor's face.

The final scene, 15 and Andrea fool the border guards into allowing him to carry the Discorsi across the border out of Italy to help spark early capitalist development. The last line:

Andrea:     We're really just at the beginning.

Ibid, p. 113.

Here Brecht is in accord with Boal (2008) does not allow the resolution or dénouement of the play, if we read it as I do as emotionally tragic. 'Aristotle's Coercive System of Tragedy' must allow the catharsis on stage for it to function and control 'spectators as an agent of social control, it fails to do so here.

In conclusion, I argue that noting the reference to Mao Tse-Tung (1937[1968]) On Contradiction in Appendix to the Short Organum, Brecht (1964) p. 278 which was a development in Marxist dialectics in which the 'first principle' relationship to its antithesis can change in the Imperialist Era. In Classical Marxism, it is proletarian to the bourgeoisie, so for Mao it becomes the oppressed to the bourgeoisie. Brecht expresses concern for:

'The over-emphasis on the principle side of the contradiction'.

Brecht (1964) p278

86

Was this a reaffirmation the State line after his 'deviation' in lending a degree of sympathy with the worker's uprising in East Berlin in 1953? I think not. To leave an unresolved thesis to the dialectic at the end of the play to be premiered by the Berliner Ensemble in Berlin in 1957 would be tantamount to saying 'really existing socialism' didn't exist, that the contradictions were not all resolved and to say the ruling bureaucracy were 'fetishized' in a 'cult of personality'. Brecht, like all great Modernists leaves his audience with a fragmented reality, an unanswered question. For Brecht it was social question to be answered by the proletarian revolution.

**Bibliography.**

Boal. A (2008) *Theatre of the Oppressed*, London: Plato Press.

Bentley. E (1998) *Bentley on Brecht*, New York: Applause.

Brecht, B (1964) *Brecht on Theatre; The Development of an Aesthetic*, ed, and trains. by J. Willett, London: Methuen.

Brecht, B (2013) *Life of Galileo*, trans. by J.Willett, ed. by J. Willett and R.Manheim, London: Methuen.

Downtown Brown, R, Gupta, S *Aesthetics and Modernism: debating twentieth Century Literature 1900-1960,* Walder, D Bertolt Brecht Life of Galileo Milton Keynes: The Open University.

Jameson. F (2000) *Brecht and Method*, New York: Verso

Gupta, S, Johnston D (2005) *A Twentieth Century Reade: Texts and Debates*, Milton Keynes, The Open University.

Nigel Pearce

Kant, E (1785]1993) Cottingham, J. *Western Philosophy: an anthology*, Oxford; Blackwell.

Keller, J (2009*) theatre & politics.* New York: Palgrave Macmillan.

Lunn. E (1984) *Marxism & Modernism; an historical study of Lukacs, Brecht, Benjamin and Adorno.* Berkley: University of California Press.

Mann, T (1998) *Meet und Vert* Bentley, E (1998) *Bentley on Brecht*, New York: Applause.

Marx, K & Engels, F (1955)   *Selected Works in Two Volumes, vol 1*, Foreign Languages Publishing House: Moscow.

Marx, K (2007*) Selected Works*, Oxford: Oxford University Press.

Mumford (2009) *Bertolt Brecht*, London: Routledge,

Serge, V (1939 [1982]) *Midnight in the Century*, Writers and Readers Publishing: London.

Tse-Tung, Mao (1937 [1968]) *On Contradiction*, Peking: Foreign Languages Press.

Unwin (1988*) A Guide to the Plays of Bertolt Brecht*, London: Methuen.

Wallis, M, Shepherd, S (2013*) Studying Plays*, London:  Bloomsbury.

**Part Two.**

**Prose Fiction.**

**Two men and a mermaid.**

'Two souls, alas, are housed within my breast.'

- Goethe.

A chill gust of wind swept frosted contorted leaves across the car park in a frenzy of colour, copper brown and red. John held on tightly to his diary, his case load was now reduced by another one. A glint of satisfaction which was almost reptilian appeared in his eyes as he glanced, no almost glared, upwards at the grey and black clouds. He pulled out a copy of Goethe, Faust from the inside pocket of his jacket, but he hardly noticed the tatty book other than to glimpse the cover subliminally. Its contents had been ingested when he was a university student. Rather, his attention was settled on the meeting that he had just left:

'Yes, that is another box ticked, empowering the clients.' He said smiling to himself.

After all, that is what it says in those shiny new social work textbooks and he is the incarnation of modern social work. That smile was so different from his clients. It exposed a perfect set of glinting teeth. Of course John cleaned his teeth twice a day and went to the dentist every six months, unlike his clients who neglected their appearance. He was a man on his way up, but to where you my reader might have wondered too, heaven?

A middle aged woman watched him; she must remain invisible to him. Her name is Angelina and she keeps copious notebooks on the social workers' interactions with his equally visible colleges and clients. She wrote on a notepad which was battered and torn that she guarded close in her inner sanctum. It is a hotchpotch of memory, observations and analysis:

> *There walks another straight-back, unburdened by life. I shall disclose a little secret which is not widely appreciated about social work, 'a box ticked' carries the same value whether it is a discharge because of some unforeseen  recovery, change in circumstances or a suicide. Why? Because there was a Third Great Depression, a reorganization of social services a contraction in welfare provision and a new phrase: 'the choice agenda.' has entered the vocabulary. This means that the clients' could make 'a choice' to jump off a multi-story car park. their responsibility, their 'choice', so you see the latter-day priest, the social worker bears no sin and he had the ultimate alibi, maybe?*

He closed the door of his car; it was secure, just like an iron womb. The 'in' ambient music of Brain Enno caresses him in full surround sound, he feels safe and significant in his world.

Then he opened the diary:

> *Pam: 10.00-10.30, [Goal, there is not anyone known to us else in bed with her.  Consider intramuscular contraception at the next team meeting.] Lunch with Luscious Lesley the new secretary.*
> *Stephen: 1.30-2.00 [Already discharged, isolated, no family, potential suicide, but intelligently competent]. Note to self, this will be seen as quite a coup. He has been on the books for years!*

And so it continued…

Angelina opened her notebook:

> *Lotta continua.*

These two words sliced like splinters of memory into her heart as she recollected those chilly hot *Brigade Rossi* days which possessed her youth.

> *How had Brigade Rossi lost, but of course we hadn't. No, it was merely a*
> *setback along the necessary road of dialectical conflicts, which*
> *Cluttered yet fuelled the route to 'actual existing socialism.'*

She paced restlessly with thoughts trapped in her head like particles in The Large Hadron Collider. Lit a cigarette, inhaled deeply and smiled at the bourgeoisie's naivety and continued to write:

> *Her comrades, those who had avoided death by the bullet, prison or long-*
> *term incarceration in psychiatric hospitals or equally had risen almost like the*
> *Nazarethian we're now in mid – life. They were scattered, some were in*
> *Trotskyist grouplets, while others had been like moles quietly burrowing into*
> *Radical churches, a few were deep Entryists, Entryism sui generis, in the arts*
> *or academia and yet others have been like her, Angelina, embedded in the*
> *Lumpenproletariat. Yes, it was a tough road for the vanguard. After all she*
> *had been incarcerated in penal institutions and then transferred to various*
> *psychiatric hospitals. She had been wired-up to the grid for quoting Mao in a*
> *Group Therapy sessions on another occasion for lambasting a charge nurse*
> *for being a 'male chauvinist pig' and standing like a slab of marble to defend*
> *black patients from racist abuse. Yes Electro Convulsive Therapy was*
> *used to 'correct deviant tendencies' by the megalomaniac doctors. It was*
> *like being given a blast of amnesia twice a week, only the strongest could*
> *resist and continue the struggle.*

Today, she conceived, she stands rather like Rosa Luxemburg, described by Clara Zetkin as 'the living flame of revolution.' She almost tore her notepad from her grey flannel jacket and wrote:

*Burn, baby, burn.*

She gripped a black pen with such passionate; she held it rigidly in her hand, which had almost become a clenched fist, that it spurted ink, the synthesis, dialectically speaking, of that particular stream within her thinking. Simultaneously, but in an almost separate reality Lesley thought that getting a petrol fuelled, testosterone driven social worker to buy her a few decent meals and a bottle or two of plonk was not a bad scheme. All the staff had monthly meals; they were supposed to be for team morale and professional bonding.

Stephen, who was recently discharged by that strutting cock of a man who glanced at Goethe while jack booting across the Social Service department car park hadn't eaten for several days. He did not keep a diary; he hadn't the need of one, but kept verse in a stash tin in a secret place and travelled light, so light, like a feather that he is blown higher and higher on the exhalations of the Earth's autumnal wind which were becoming icy winds and gales of winter. He plummeted one morning and then he realized help was much needed. There were none so he went to see 'the Man', the dealer.

Angelina was whispering about with her notepad when she clocked the young man rolling one spliff more than was good for him, spaced-out is not adequate to describe his state of mind; zonked but conscious seemed to be rather a more suitable assessment she decided:

'Hey cat, where do you live, where's your pad.' She spoke with kindness.

'Hi, are you some Madonna.'

'No.' she laughed, 'No, not me.'

She realized this was the first time she had laughed spontaneously for a long time.

'I thought you were Our Lady of The Angels, come to take me higher. To hold me in your arms and escort me to heaven.' He grinned.

'Hey babe Icarus, now don't get to fly too close to heaven. It might not be what you expect. But where do to you crash, the 'heat' will pull you, be careful.'

'Nowhere.'

She carefully removed her grey flannel jacket, an old companion, and wrapped it around the shoulders of the young man; she held him in her arms and by the rocking rhythm of a lullaby soothed him. There was not an alternative, he needed shelter and she took him to her nest, an anonymous flat in a grey concrete block where the State housed those on 'benefits'. Inside the sparsely furnished one bedroom flat was a disproportionately large collection of books. They were on shelves built with wooden planks resting on reddish house bricks which formed columns at each end, but the books still overflowed onto the floor. She possessed no cooker, but a kettle and an old microwave to heat food. Purple drapes were hung permanently across the small windows. The interior light was provided by unshaded electric fitments. She laid cushions on the floor of the area which doubled up for a kitchen and a library and lowered him onto this bed; he was almost comatose with the amount of skunk he had smoked and hashish cookies that he had gobbled. Although she knew his life was not at risk, you don't O.D on cannabis, but you can take it too far. She removed her jacket from his body and covered his ragged clothes with a thick red covering which had green and blue mermaids embroidered on them.

'Babe Icarus, you glide down softly.' She whispered.

He was unconscious for forty-eight hours and Angelina was awake and alert for the whole of those two days and nights. She wandered around whipping the sweats from his body like a moth drawn to a flickering light.

'Hi, who are you, where am I. I mean how did I get here.'

'Stoned and incapable.' Smile Angelina.

A hot flush of embarrassment coloured the young man's face....

'Don't worry, babe Icarus, you were too stoned to walk let alone anything else. The police would have picked you-up and there were several sticks of skunk not so carefully popping out of your socks. Do you want something to eat?'

'Yes, yes, please, very much.'

'See that rectangular brown thing and a small oblong of lighter stuff. It is bread and cheese, help yourself. Those blue things to your right are jeans which should fit you and the white thing next to it is a cheesecloth shirt. See you in ten.'

'Oh yes?' He wondered.

Angelina and the young man began to write a web of words within this flat. Would it be a drama, a Comedy, Tragedy, a tragicomedy? Possibly a pot-boiler of a romance or a piece of Socialist Realism, they could write a life of mystery and fable because this flat was a veritable laboratory of the creative mind: a cauldron of the emotions. However, we know Angelina has a secret notebook and the young man hides his writing in a stash box. She knew his was inviolable when she had laid him down for his slumber; she would never, ever, lift the lid off this box and delve within. It was his sanctum, his mind's temple. They conversed carefully, feeling and then plucking strings of the instrument which they were tuning into a relationship:

'I don't know your name.'

'Either do I.' She replied.

'That's a funny answer, do you always talk in riddles.'

'That is no riddle, babe Icarus. '

'That's my new name, is it?'

'Maybe so.'

'Okay'

'That's settled then, you have been named!'

'Okay, boss' he smiled

She grimaced and flinched:

'Never, every call me "boss" again, you understand that. Never ever use that filthy word to describe me, anyone, but them and their lackeys.'

'What's wrong, I was joking.'

'Jokes are not always just what they seem. Have you read Freud *Jokes and Their Relationship to the Unconscious*?'

'Heavy stuff. You are not like one of the shrinks, which we used to see or those social workers. You know when they smile you first see perfect teeth, but the mirage wears off, then you see their fangs.'

'I am sorry, babe Icarus. No, I am not a shrink or a social worker. Here, have you ever worn a kaftan, one would suit you.'

She pops into her bedroom produces one like a magician (it was really quite a relic she had dragged around on her wanderings since the 1970's). She held it, measuring it in front of him for size:

'Hey, you will make a hippie yet.'

And they both smile, hugging each other as if they had been lost in a labyrinth and finally found a companion to help them escape or at least to accompany one another on those interminable journeys which exist within any maze.

She writes once again in her journal, recalling a quote from Albert Camus which she inscribes slowly and contemplatively, like a nun in an enclosed convent:

*"Autumn is a second spring when every leaf is a flower.'.    - Albert Camus."*

Life in the flat did not fall into a dull routine of revolutionary inculcation, they had fallen in love. True, Angelina had always been in love with the revolution and was devoted to the 'struggle'. 'Babe Icarus' was a young man of visions and voices who had been unloved, but she would come to realize that she cannot reciprocate his love for too long. Though she knew could never tell him why, it was because she was and will always be *Brigade Rossi,* the ramifications would be potentially unmanageable. She and Babe Icarus would be on the run from both friends and enemies. caught-up in a cross-fire of intrigue, he would never cope she calculated. However, this ballet, this Prokofiev ballet, which is like the Shakespearian drama, it took from it because Angelina and 'Babe Icarus' were indeed "star crossed lovers", but also Angelina was a child of the inheritance of October 1917.

She probed a little into the dark night of his mind, could it resembles 'the dark night of the soul' and anticipate a higher state of ecstasy. She was willing to listen:

'Babe Icarus, tell me about those visions and voices. What the shrinks call your illness, is it Schizophrenia.'

'It isn't really an illness at all, you see. I am both blessed and damned in equal measure like William Blake was; Blake lives in me. I am also the Fallen Angel from Milton, Paradise *Lost* and because I descended into *The Inferno* of Dante so I always say: 'Abandon hope, all you who enter here.'

'Babe Icarus, I wouldn't 'tell' you what to do, but possibly the skunk and the hashish for some people are not the best if they have certain proclivities. Marx said:

'Religion is the opium of the people, it is the sign of the

oppressed creature.'

He fell silent, and marched out of the room. A gradual, but discernible change occurred from then onwards. They were after all of different Houses: the Capulets and Montagues, so it follows her being a revolutionary damaged by the system she had attempted to overthrow, but he was well different she thought infatuated with the distorted image of the 'self'. She then realized 'Babe Icarus' was a narcissist of sorts, but one that hated his own refection although could not free himself of the bondage of staring at his own mental deformities. So she could never tell him her truth and he was in love, not with her but his malady…

Late-autumn became mid-winter; Angelina knew there would be no thaw. She penned in her diary:

*This shall be the winter of our discontents.*

But either forgetfully or with subconsciously with intent did not place it in is hiding place. She went into the other room to make a coffee while he exchanged rooms apparently to lie-down:

'Angelina, what is this book I found on the bed.'

'Oh, I don't know, you tell me. Explain it to me, and then I shall ravish both your analysis and you.'

'What is *Brigade Rossi?'* Does it mean Red Brigade, no not those, not those terrorists?

She froze as surely as if struck by a bolt of ice, she shattered fragments melted in the heat of rage, tears boiled, poured out of her eyes with uncontrollable body jerking sobs:

'No, never, we were not 'terrorists.''

Confused, he rushed out of the flat without dressing, screaming through the network of streets to the Social Services Department. It was locked as it always for security reasons, staff safety, but there was no one at the reception desk just a note taped across the intercom:

**We are sorry, there is no one available at present, please ring and leave a message and we will get back to you as soon as possible.**

It was the monthly staff meal... Stephan then ran to the Roman Catholic Church; but a note had been permanently attached to the church door months earlier, the rain had defaced it slightly. There was no Eucharistic Meal to be eaten there for the priests had left:

**Mass cancelled due to a shortage of priests. You are in always in our prayers. In an emergency, seek appropriate help from the Social Services or dial 999.**

The young man thought it read 666 and it was the code from The Book of Revelation of the Antichrist. It would be stamped upon his forehead. He became totally deranged and threatened to burn down both the Social Services Department and the Church, a passer-by made a mobile for calls to the police who by procedure alerted the psychiatric team. The social worker arrived first; he had rushed to get there because he had discharged the young man and wanted to get there before the police. Angelina also arrived, breathless, and confronted him; she pulled out a small black Lugar pistol with what seemed a blur of dark grey:

'Now just give me that gun. Steady, you must be ill, a very poorly woman.'

'Don't patronize me. My name is Angelina, I am a revolutionary and you are a pig, a muttonhead. You will never put him back in that place, the so-called hospital.'

She pulled the trigger again and again and yet again, emptying the small magazine:

'Now, that is another box ticked don't you think, ah.'

And spits onto the hunched figure of the moaning figure and then calmly walked away like a whisper into the wind.

Days later the papers reported a suicide. Another had jumped from Beachy Head onto those rocks which are pounded by a relentless and remorseless sea. The body or what remained of it after however long it was thrashed by the sea was torn, bloated and blue. A note had found nearby the cliff edge hidden under a bush and weighed down with a stone. There was simply inscribed in small, neat handwriting:

"My name is Legion, for we are many.' - Mark 5:9.'

It was rumoured by some that a mermaid could be seen; she swam around the cliffs ceaselessly, carelessly without concern and gambled with the waves as they crashed onto those wailing, desirous and deadly rocks.

**Reflections on the story.**

Four areas were foremost in my mind as I wrote *Two Men and a Mermaid*. The first was concentrating on an emphasis on the interactions between plot, character and setting, these three elements. Secondly, I was aware of the requirement to 'show not tell' and tried to move towards this aim. Thirdly, I was interested in the relationship between *Socialist Realism* in Babel (1940) *The Red Cavalry and Other Stories* and origins of the short-story in fable. Finally, I noted the significance of the Edgar Allen Poe theory of the 'unity of effect' on the short story and attempted to implement some of his guidance.

My narrator's point of view is third-person omniscient. A device I used was the insertion of the written material of my characters into the story, an epistolary dimension. This seemed a useful method to help create 'round' characters. Thus the narrate gains a more intimate insight into the characters, especially Angelina, through diary entries which by their nature are first person direct narration and they also play a significant role in the plot. I begin *in medias res*, however the action takes place within a controlled and tight period of time and space. An awareness of the oral origins of the short story, let to the use of a 'framing device' with the social worker's entry and his assassination. I conclude with the mermaid whose appearance is almost Magical Realist in nature and is intended to defamiliarize.

The image of the 'black-pen' and equally black 'Lugar pistol' is phallic, thus questioning conventional gender roles in Angelina, but also modes of 'expression' for her creativity. She is the Dialectic incarnate, both creative and destructive. Her 'epiphany' which has its origins in Joyce (1914) *Dubliners* take place when she falls in 'love', but it is a tragic love because of her previous involvement with the Red Brigades in Italy. Like Juliet she cannot escape her past (familial or ideological. She could never share this secret with 'babe Icarus' because he is vulnerable. He finds her diary and reads it. He sees her involvement with Red Brigades as e 'fatal flaw. Indeed, her murder of the social worker is ideologically consistent; an agent of what Louis Althusser called the 'Repressive State Apparatus' while patrolling the 'Ideological State Apparatus'. He could have admitted 'babe Icarus' into a psychiatric hospital, which also conflicts with her historic anti-psychiatry beliefs. She is left in crisis, but because there is nowhere for her go to find fulfilment, there is no 'actual existing socialism' and hence her denouncement can only be a transformation into a mythological creature, half woman, half fish who must gamble with death by riding the rollers onto the rocks by Beachy Head. Like Sophocles *Antigone, she* has acted against the State and her punishment is like being entombed alive in the body of a mermaid..

# The Flight of Icarus

**Janet, you were on my mind.**

..."if you can't adapt yourself to living in a mental hospital how do

you expect to be able to live 'out in the world'?" How indeed?"

— Frame (2012) p.34.

The mists were leaden with the hum of significance, a salience of silence. A cave, a fire and some shadows lingered beyond the cave. However, as in Plato's allegory only the 'philosophers' were privileged to see the shadows, the 'Forms'. I had an intense interest in abstractions. Nevertheless, I pulled the heavy burgundy velvet curtains of my study closed. it was a foggy, chilly twilight and the screams of my patients were reverberating in my head. The year was 1957, the country New Zealand and the hospital Seacliff Lunatic Asylum. I treated one young woman patient who had been a student teacher, an undisclosed, at the time, aspirin overdose. She had continued to university where she wrote a story about her depressive breakdown. her English lecturer who she was infatuated with, or so the notes say, showed it to one of my superiors at this asylum and so would begin an odyssey. Janet Frame had been detained in in 1952; I was to meet her nearly five benumbed years later.

I had a call from Auckland six months before I met Janet, followed by a paper chase of correspondence, but I reached the end. I was awarded funding to head a programme into Rehabilitation and Creativity. For me it was like Manna had started falling from Heaven. However, all that seemed possible in the short term were incremental changes to the system and some basic activities. Weaving and assembling stools, free expression art classes and the beginnings of a group of handpicked patients who would use Freudian 'free association' to create a group poem or story. The patients in this group would be pre-surgery. I was given free rein

103

and of course an ex-undergraduate, however disturbed the patient, and seemed an ideal candidate. and so I met 'an angel at my table', Janet Frame, apparently a fledgling author. I sought out Miss Frame. She was huddled in the corner of a padded isolation cell, a padded cell. She looked like a bird that had flown into a plane of glass blinded by a snowstorm, injured, bewildered and frightened. She seemed a broken person: teeth pulled out, ill-fitting dentures, ulcers around her mouth, but had with an uncontrollable mop of red hair. I was now a little further up their Tower of Babel, a senior registrar. This provided me with a certain degree of autonomy. Although I couldn't challenge the demigods, the consultants, I could not make decisions independently of them.

'Miss Frame, um, may I address you… Janet,' I said tentatively.

'I don't want it., I don't love paraldehyde, they said Shelia did and then she died.'

'Janet, I am so sorry about your friend.'

'She wasn't my friend, but they killed her. It was wrong.'

I felt like the collective hand of the patients was going to slap me. What could I say…? An uneasy silence filled the vacuum between us, but at least that was a beginning, I thought. Better than the descent into the inferno. You can fill a vacuum, with something; respect, compassion, even friendship.

'They call me an educated bitch.'

'That is unfortunate, Janet, but not all the patients are as well read, as educated as you. You mustn't take offence…'

'No, the nurses do.'

Unprepared my response was one of incredulity, then sympathy for this sad woman.

'Do you hear many voices, Janet, like God or Keats? Emily Dickinson, maybe? Your fellow writers?'

'Fool', she screamed. 'but you are no "Holy Fool" in rags.'

'Nurse, Sister - quickly, restrain her, then the medicine, the usual dose, it will have been written up in her notes.' I reacted robotically.

I nipped into the doctor's consulting room, took a small leather lined hip flask from one pocket and had a quick gulp of the medicine, the whisky, and a peppermint popped a peppermint into my mouth almost simultaneously with the other hand. My hands were trembling.

Janet's consultant prescribed a course of E.C.T after this incident. It seemed inappropriate to me, almost punitive. No patient reacts well when their symptoms are challenged. It is like challenging someone's Weltanschauung, something the most stable person would find unsettling one way or another. This was hardly the therapeutic beginning I had hoped for; I had not anticipated it. To be absolutely honest, I was angry with the male consultant: he seemed to be trying to impinge on my programme. It was a question of professional boundaries, or so I thought. Now I was doubly motivated, my engines were in gear and smoking: my project and my professional pride. I knew this was a pivotal moment in my chosen career, but I hadn't realized it would become something of an 'Epiphany, of course not of the magnitude of a James Joyce text. After all, this wasn't Dublin and so the literary academics were saying in those quasi-literary journals, Modernism if not dead, was in decline. I had a predilection for the short story...

Have you read Ward No.6? just checking you, my reader, the author's name was on the tip of my tongue, blazes, how on earth could I forget, the master: yes, that was it: Anton Chekhov. He is the weaver of my nightmares. I am haunted by Chekhov's character Ivan Gromov. I have been since I read that damned book. Why am I to be nailed to a cross as surely as Jesus of Nazareth was crucified upon one by that particular spectre of Chekhov's mind, Gromov, after all I am no Dr. Ragin? I am a doctor though, but I did not intend being admitted to my own asylum. How the hell did Chekhov conjure that up? Seacliff Lunatic Asylum has its own little cherry orchard, but it does blossom, frost had eaten it years before... A community where the walls were wobbling with weeping and wailing, not that the walls had been built in no less a sturdy fashion as than the average monastery. So robust that not many patients left; even if they did, stupefied into submission by the great machine of cogs and wheels of the institution, they would be unable to compete in the tragedy of a society with its cash-nexus and mind ant marching conformity. I can tell you that many of my patients were not clinically ill, but people whose face didn't fit the necessary identikit picture at the right time. A crash, a clap of thunder heralded a downpour. Evening deepened and I poured the first shot of that whisky which was my anaesthesia, then a second and when I woke in bed with a hangover, there was no memory of leaving my study to the quarters attached. For, yes, we doctors also lived in the asylum, but in houses, not dormitories.

I was beginning to have to justify the funding for my project; it had begun to look overly ambitious. Yes, I had a stockroom of wooden stools with woven seats, piles of randomly bespattered paper, the artwork, but nothing which was going to get me really noticed, nothing for the CV which would clinch a consultant's post. Of all the patients there was the only one whom I knew that had a history of writing: Janet. I parachuted down from my deluded heights and I realized the magnitude of my task. 900Nine hundred patients, drugged to the point of stupefaction;, insulin therapy had wreaked havoc;, E.C.T being used as a method of control, indeed in some cases as punishment and also there was a culture amongst the majority of consultants of wait, then wait again and then apply the scalpel to make them free. Where were they

106

when the news of the medical experimentation on patients in Nazi Germany was seeping out after the Nuremburg Trails? I couldn't get the analogy out of my mind between 'Cut makes free' and the motto above the concentration camps 'Work makes free.' Yes, they were using the lobotomy and leucotomy on a routine basis. Women looked dazed, blank, with brightly coloured headscarves; it had a resemblance of Dante's, Inferno. I saw the words drip off the scalpel I had handed the consultant two days previously:

No room for hope, when you enter this place.

Dante (2008) p.56.

Janet would eventually be lobotomized; I could save her and get some decent writing, which would justify my Rehabilitation and Creativity Programme. She wouldn't be discharged, that much was obvious to me, but she would write. That would tick the necessary boxes and avoid her surgery and my career and conscience were boosted. I was saved.

'If you pumped too much gas into a balloon, it would burst. Splat!'
Who said that? I shuddered, but 'The Madman' continued,

'God is dead. God remains dead. And we have killed him. How shall we comfort ourselves, the murderers of all murderers?'

Was that Nietzsche's spectre raised to haunt me?

'The Madman 'noted on his pad of dust that Janet's family had stopped visiting long ago;, it was a long journey after all and the doctors always know what is for the best, the parents thought. Janet was quite happy; they had been assured, years ago. She had lost siblings in freak accidents. However, there was a younger sister who had graduated and married; she began to see dark clouds in this apparently benign forecast. She had lodged with Janet at one time, just when her older sister was apparently going insane; Janet had not seemed crazy to her. A little odd, maybe, but that was Janet. and this diagnosis, once she and her husband really applied themselves to the research, did not quite fit, and in fact into seemed wrong. Schizophrenia: it just did not make sense. The sister had known Janet wrote short-stories and, overcoming some resistance from mother and father, she rummaged, searched and sought them out. Eureka! She had found Janet's notebooks, now to read them and then show them to her husband. It could be nonsense, ravings; perhaps they were right and she was wrong. They was only one way to discover the truth: read them, show them to old teachers , perhaps not that lecturer who had Janet 'committed' 'for a little rest' and maybe then send them away to a competition or to a publisher or something. Any clue to find out what might have happened to her sister and then take action. this atrophy was unbearable. Janet's life was not a stagnant pool covered with algae, at least it hadn't been. The 'Mad Man' wrote.

I, The doctor wondered if like Dr. Ragin iwi was beginning to loose 'the plot', should there be a 'plot' as Aristotle claimed; or was I living in a different genre, the short-story, which may be like the 1950's and life generally without a 'purpose', perhaps it is a 'seamless plot', or a tranche de vie. A doctor is not a 'free man' and must as unfree men everywhere be trapped in the 'plot' as Woolf realized that only: if he 'were a free man rather than a slave... there would be no plot.' Now back to the 'plot', against me? No, I meant Aristotle: I shall, indeed insist have 'a beginning, middle and an end'. The place to find the plot as every psychiatrist knows is in the notes written by other psychiatrists -, the voice of the plot, of Reason. However, any writings by Janet remained only referred to, but were not actually present. What the hell? no, keep your head; have a slug of whisky.

'The Mad Man' had contrived a plot., her sister would be its agent for Janet and her sister just as Antigone and her brother shared the same 'blood', the same inheritance. Now was the time for to implement it, conjuring up a spell of purple haze which would transmute into a flying carpet carrying Janet's golden words. Janet's sister had read a notebook of her short stories and discussed them with her husband. They decided to send the collection off to a National Short story competition. it was a high risk strategy, but there seemed little choice as it was spring 1957 and Janet had been held incommunicado for years without any visitors.

It was a very hot summer and the patients were roasting and becoming agitated. The heat was on me to deliver on this project; a lot depended on it, my career. The scalpels were being whirled in an almost frenzy now. the Head of Psychiatry had had a taste of blood, and thought he had solved the enigma. A new surgical unit was being built to increase the production of the 'cure', 'lobotomize them, and leucotomize them.' was the Master Plan., that is the final solution;, the best made plans can go astray, solutions can have their test tubes broken and leak out to corrode the scientists, the doctors, even contaminated them.

The 'madman' noted the short story collection was like a spear thrown into the heart of psychiatry. it won the first prize: Miss Janet Frame was a nationally recognized writer. The scales were not only unbalanced, they had collapsed. Our progressive doctor, - that's right, the one so concerned about his patients that he had to self-medicate with whisky - was going to be the lamb that would be sacrificed. The consultants would use that incident in the padded cell. after all the ward Sister had heard him accuse Janet of hearing voices and sanctioned the injection. It was a stitch-up. Chekhov was indeed a master of the short story and knew the human condition; well, not exactly Ward No. 6, but too damned close for the doctor's sanity.

He would be found years later in a cave in Thailand with an unlimited supply of opium supplied by whom...? He would puff on his hooker enter reveries and tell strange tales of a mental hospital, a Russian writer and a woman who became a significant writer he had once treated and cured. No-one thought these stories made sense: it was the opium and a touch of madness people said. He neglected his appearance and lived in the tattered rags of a 'Holy Fool.'

'The Madman' gleefully wrote that at Seacliff Lunatic Asylum, the consultants were feverish; Janet's sister and husband were due with copies of the book for Janet to sign. Nothing for it but to put her on an open ward.

"Miss Frame, there appears to have been a mistake, an erroneous diagnosis by a senior doctor, but not a consultant, you understand. Your book has won a National competition and you are to be discharged."

'No more injections, no more .E.C.T.'

'Janet, you are to be discharged into the care of your sister and her husband. We wish you every success.'

'Oh, I see,' Janet smiled dubiously.

The 'open' ward was a very different story; it had a different 'plot' and denouncement. There was no paraldehyde there, you know, of course, or maybe not, wrote 'The Madman' in his pad of dust, that they have to administer it in glass syringes as it melts plastic ones. The characters were also different than on the 'closed' wards, deep in the dark heart of this place where there is no light. The patients here are overly stressed housewives and politely spoken shopkeepers speaking platitudes. They gave these patients, those chalky little yellow helpers, and diazepam. Fresh flowers were placed in porcelain vases every day and there was much, to Jean's relief, decent food. The nurses smiled and there were not thorns, but

Colgate gleaming teeth. I can lap this up, wrote Janet in her the newly acquired book for her writing the ward sister had given her. But, the dream has been, as always, disturbed by the nasty little business: waking reality. These patients stayed a maximum of three months and the headlights of the sister's husband's car was driving through the night with the two convinced they were knights saving Jane from the darkest of nights.

'The Madman' closed his pad of dust and sprinkled it on Antigone's brother's corpse. For this story of blood and was also about inheritance, a tale of madness and sanity, of corruption and purity. It is not the biography of Janet Frame., yes, the dates were correct and the basic facts were correct, but it is the creation of an imagination who found an inspiration in the story of Miss Janet Frame., 'The Madman' contrived with Janet's sister and unhinged the doctor. Why, because every suicide of people 'The Madman' had known was etched on his heart in golden script., he had not forgotten or forgiven their tormentors until their unquiet spirits would be at rest. He pondered that Janet had flown into the cage they placed his mind into. Yes, he was also restrained and had involuntary E.C.T as a young person; he also wrote finding a path out of the psychiatric hospital through publication and academic study. The caged bird sings and sings when he or she is freed and quite often those who had locked the gilded cage did not like to hear what was said about them. However, you cannot silence a song, a story or a poem, however, particularly after it is published. It is a biographical fact that the New Zealand psychiatric authorities would not let Janet Frame 'go', even in death. One analysis of her writing claimed she had Borderline Personality Disorder. The Madman smiles and thinks if she were alive, she would retort:

'No, I an m not like you.'

**Bibliography.**

Chekhov, A (2003) Seven Short Novels, New York: W.W. Norton & Company

Dante, A (2008) The Divine Comedy, Oxford: Oxford World Classics

Frame, J (2012) Faces in the Water, London: Virago Modern Classics.

Kaufmann, W (1969) Existentialism from Dostoevsky to Sartre, Cleveland & Ohio: Meriden Books.

## Reflections on the story

Frank O'Conner noted:

> In discussions of the modern novel, we have come to talk
> as if the novel is without a hero. In fact the short story had
> a hero. What it had was a submerged population group-.

O'Conner (2004) p.14.

This was my starting point; short-stories are about 'outsiders'. The discussion in (in Gebbie (2013) pp. 134-138) of *One Flew Over the Cuckoo's Nest* provided a theme or 'premise' for my short story. One recurring 'motif' in the work is the nature of Aristotle's discussion of the nature of 'plot'. My story is as much about the nature of writing in post-modernity while looking at Modernism as it is about psychiatric hospitals. I also was interested in 'death of the God' and its consequences for universe 'Form' which I comment on in the first paragraph. The Madman quotes Nietzsche; this is the actual 'climax' or 'turning point'. Nietzsche (1969) attributed the quote to a 'Madman'. All unravels after this: I try to 'show' as well as 'tell' the disintegration. A denouncement with the doctor back in Plato's Cave smoking opium and the Madman smiles' as Janet condemns psychiatry from the grave.

I attempted to write this story is written from two P.O.V's:., the doctor, is a First-Person Narrator, we hear his interior monologue; and 'The Madman', a Third Person Limited Omniscient Narrator.: The doctor and 'The Madman' as are competing P.O.V's as well too as characters make conflict inherent in the structure of my story, although there are also secondary conflicts, i.e. between the doctor and his superiors in the pecking order, of course Janet and the psychiatric system.

An inspiration for the whole endeavour came from Virginia Woolf's 1925 essay, *Modern Fiction* in which she commented on the relationship between writers and 'Form':

> ...if he could base his work upon his own feeling and not upon
> conventions, there would be no plot, no comedy, no tragedy, no
> love interest or catastrophe in the accepted style...

Hunter (2007) p.64.

The Doctor quotes an extract in the story as he contemplates the nature of 'plot'.

Of course an attempt to merge Dr. Rabin and Ivan Gromov from Chekhov's Ward No.6 with the Doctor and 'The Madman' was pure enjoyment. This is also an aspect of my attempt to continue to comment on the short story as 'form' by merging one into another with as few seams as possible. I use the metaphor of words 'dripping' as if blood from the doctor's scalpel. The epigram from Frame (2012) Faces in the Water is both a 'hook' and it 'foreshadows' the resolution, 'How indeed' could one survive in a dysfunctional society if you cannot cope with life in the mental hospital. Janet Frame, in my story, remains unbroken by psychiatry and speaks from beyond the grave on the transmutation of her diagnosis from Schizophrenia to Borderline Personality Disorder; perhaps she had been just a little eccentric. An element of my critique or 'premise' is the tendency to make the whole of society pathological. It is worthy to note that Freud had warned of the perils of 'folk psychology' (Davidson, 1999 pp 106-6) i.e. psychoanalysis practiced by those with no or inadequate training.

**Bibliography**.

Aristotle (1996) Poetics, London: Penguin Classics.

Chekhov, A. (2003) Seven Short Novels., New York: W.W. Norton & Company

Frame, J. (2012) Faces in the Water. London: Virago Modern Classics.

Gebbie, V. (2013)    Short Circuit: A Guide to the Art of the Short Story. Norfolk: SALT.

Hunter, A. (2007) The Cambridge Introduction to The Short Story in English, Cambridge: Cambridge University Press.

Kaufmann, W. (1969) Existentialism from Dostoevsky to Sartre, Cleveland & Ohio: Meriden Books.

Lodge, D. (1992) The Art of Fiction, London, Penguin Books

O'Conner, F. (2004) The Lonely Voice: A Study of the Short Story, New Jersey: Melville House Classics.

Smith, D.L, (1999) Freud's Philosophy of the Unconscious, Netherlands: Kluwer Academic Publishers.

**A Story on the writing of a story.**

If he could base his work upon his own feeling and
not upon conventions, there would be no plot, no
comedy, no tragedy, no love interest or catastrophe
in the accepted style...

- Virginia Woolf's (1925), *Modern Fiction.*

Reflecting, he remembered he should make a plan for his short story. As he did for his life, indeed for everything. He was kneeling before a blank page and had intended racing across it a roar of triumph. His intellect a triumph to his ego. Yes, at last the world would understand the genius within him. A faltering attempt, then racing he must catch-up he must outshine all the other writers. What other writers? Well, there was... especially but also... and then that... He would become a beacon, shrine before all who would have to prostrate themselves. His parent's, elderly, didn't really like to contradict him and his brother was fed up with the hassle. He had made a pass at a young lesbian nurse and then had not regretted it. As he did not know she was gay. And he loved to portray himself as this knight on a white charger coming to the rescue of all women, but with the secret ambition of sleeping with them. She would not forget and the 'system' would wash their hands of him. There was a Section 3, so there were also Section 117 obligations. He was oblivious to her as he was about most other human beings. In fact, he was an android who dreamed of electric sheep. He thought he would compete with his most imitated adversary and, try for some anti-depressants on top of his anti-psychotic medicine. He told the psychiatrist that he felt 'flat'. The nurse intervenes like a panther in the night and suggests they reduce his anti-psychotics to elevate that 'flatness' and then says she has read his notes. There was never a diagnosis made, he has been in hospital only

116

twice and she suggests exaggerated his condition. Doctor Feel-Nothing realizes he has been taken for a ride and doesn't like it. The six month discharge plan put into place. All those copies of those books sent to top publishers are returned with polite notes into his inbox. Oh dear, looks like it's a life in the Cosmic Allotment where he is the Divine Gardner. Oh well, we all make mistakes... He doesn't though, he thinks to himself, now this next story will do it!

### Doctor Death is calling', my friend said.

The room had not been cleaned since this speed binge began nine months previously. It was a mess, orange juice cartons as we believed that the Vitamin would keep us well, that was a fallacy. Mainlining over, well over a gram of high quality Amphetamine Sulphate every day with an assortment of hallucinogens it was becoming very surreal indeed. I saw many things as the walls weaved around the naked bulbs. A man jacked-up a straight gram flushed [filled the syringe with blood after injecting] leapt-up and squirted the blood on the ceiling. Didn't think that was 'together' in the least. Another person, skeletal, had a blanket over his head and was hunched in the corner only coming out for a fix'. 'This is a crazy scene man', I thought. ' It is 'far out' one voice shouts, 'no man far-in, man, it's far-in.' 'Did you see the cool aura on that dog last night.' a young, we were all young, woman says. They were no dogs in the 'shooting gallery! However, there are several broken syringes lying about clogged with dark red congealed blood. I had seen a few days previously someone 'doing-up' another speed freak, but some debris was lodged in the needle, he just keeps pushing and pushing, No could move, we were memorized. Eventually the solution splattered backwards into his face. This was becoming just too 'crazy, man.'

Then, a friend who I had discussed everything from the teachings of the Buddha to the philosophy of Nietzsche over the years. Started preparing a batch of hits, proceeding around the room, injecting people saying as he pushed the plunger in:

'Hey man, this is Doctor Death calling.'

**Part Three.**

**POEMS.**

Nigel Pearce

**Leucotomy haiku [revised].**

#1

This sun wept its rays

That summer, hell bubbled hot

But no cut was made.

#2

Blister wept septic

Autumn, should have it removed

The surgeon had said.

#3

When winter came though

Ice cut my heart, it is hard

Lance with a  scalpel.

# The Flight of Icarus

**For Sylvia Plath.**

I am resting in your grave of nettles,

Your purple soul weaves it entrance,

Like an enchanted violin it is played,

By the nectar breath of your mouth.


My living willow is in a sullen tomb,

It is alight with colour and matter,

It is animated by wandering sighs,

Flowing in a purple force, my blood.


So you stroke like a lover, my pen,

I write on pages midsummer frost.

Nigel Pearce

**Whisky and Downers, age twelve.**

Just a slanted second memory of a morning,

Demons in my mind and a devil in the loins,

Empty whiskey bottle from last night's plight,

When I ride those golden waves I am surfing,

A soul was bathed in Southern Comfort bliss,

This mystery was poured with whisky gulped,

Compounded by Nitrazepam with flop and fall,

An oblivion may transcend the gift of Morpheus,

Safe, deaf, blind and with a deafening darkness,

Whisky and downers drown the mind in silence.


Observed the technique in the house called home,

The home was to be a hospital named Hollymoor.

Paper Tigers and Poets.

***Some lines composed on meeting a woman who wears a hijab,***
The reptiles are sweating with the blood of the incinerated innocents,
Their darting tongues pierce night as the drones fly over sad Arabia,
Seem to be a bit like armadillos, small armoured animals in the U.S,
An armadillo is a steel-clad animal, but is not immune from assault.

These running dogs of imperialism are bloated floating paper-tigers,
Are doomed to roar burn and be burnt 'TIGER, tiger burning bright',
This is no Crusade or Jihad; they lost to the red masses in Vietnam,
Wherever dollar, pound, franc remains King there will be resistance.

Odd Americans in rodeo cowboy hats, their steak is burnt by napalm,
They slither through the grass, snake glinting in the sun so cold eyed,
There is little grass in the desert, the Yankee snakes are dehydrated,
A taxidermist of History prepares them for last sundown in sun dune.

Poets are neither the fighters nor the swollen-foot black-booted soldiers.
Poetry's ancient aura dissolved in 'the mechanical age of reproduction',
Not shaman, but aesthetic-propagandist agent and observer of History,
Poets are 'tribunes of the oppressed', priests of souls in lost phantoms.

You, small round women in a hijab you conceal nothing but a torn heart,
One that beats with the twin drums of injustice and a love for all people.

### Housing Blues.

There was a girl without bright eyes, who contrived to see all, to be all

The family crest: 'all for one and one for all' is slightly tainted perhaps,

Since was told of a crime which would consume many, but maybe that

Person just wove fabrics of falsehoods in order to tear or sully fine lace.


There was a girl without eyes who would like to be omniscient, a priestess

Of sorts sadly a sullen racist, but lies are blown as leaves in the wild wind,

I know what a gossip here blurts out to anyone without the required senses,

Innuendo, fantasies, malice; she said some years ago she wanted me out.


The mum leads me down to a dungeon of cuckoo clocks hot butter muffins,

Here is a girl with lovely guide-guard dog named 'Sadie' she sat on my feet,

'Did you this... did you that... were you the other' Mother enquires, I had on

My university graduate fleece which seemed to throw the plans into disarray.


There was a girl, who is partially sighted although she had seen and felt much,

Thought a distance from so far North to relocate here so the adrenaline splattered,

Get up to go then the curtain lifts in the theatre *Enter girl:* 'What is Nigel doing?'

# The Flight of Icarus

*Mother:* 'He is getting up.' 'What is Nigel doing!?' 'He is just getting-up.' I flee


Feared to have that mud thrown again in these flats, yes the gossip sits twanging

Strings, playing cards, I have seen her deck before and those cards were marked,

I do not think a Tarot pack suit a sad Madonna, became a grotesque Magdalene,

Let heart of that green-eyed monster gnaw into her entrails became an art of lies,


Those serpents just twisted her dreams and clouded the clarity of her diamonds.

Nigel Pearce

**Storm and Desert.**

The fiery worms which burrowed into my mind,

Are like the maggots which are eating the soul,

Now they have died, drowned in a dark ocean,

Which raged until evaporated by the biting sun?

That tempest has lulled and my thirst has abated.

**MIND CLOCK.**

Integrating like the hands of a clock,

Pointing to the misty time of no hours,

Which passes its breath in the silence,

Slowly returning to the house of a self,

Here are shifting sands, a wilderness,

And the clock has melted with a heat,

Forget to tock in time with the Rhyme.

Nigel Pearce

**Morphine Love.**

A morphine angel stroked my mind,

As a mother rocks her child to sleep,

And a lover touched the soft breast,

Like dew on the grass in mornings,

No chaos, just the gentlest whisper,

Love between sheets of dark death.

**Heroin.**

I shot a dream up my aching arms,

In a haze of mind just lost in a skull,

Calling names from my quivering lips,

Pastel shades soothed weeping eyes,

Heaven strolls like floating lilac lilies,

In that caressed pool of emptiness,

Forgetting the anguish of our hunger,

Go those thunderclaps in our minds,

We were at peace a dewy humming.

**It is alright babe.**

The needle pieces that loving vein,

Like Love smoothing a lover's hair,

The white-heat rushes up our arm,

Into welcoming minds like sunrise.


Cruising with sleep forgotten eyes,

I watched 'the Man' as he grinned,

He had shaken-up into the kitchen,

Nobody else has clocked his move,

I just rise and stumble gaining focus,

Walk with amphetamine confidence,

A crookery-high piled shooting room,

Gently approach and smiling, saying,

'It's alright babe, give me that knife,

I have Valium in my pocket so relax,

Swallow four of them with water, relax.'


I groove back into to the music room,

# The Flight of Icarus

He finds my lost vein and another hit,

Tears have burnt farrows into my face,

It was alright babe, because of Valium.

**Gather the Fragments.**

Like a brown and ruddy crinkled autumn leaf

Blown, swept by gales, tempests and storms,

With others gushed like the chilliest hurricane,

Demand you will experience equally the puss

Perpetually

Like looking

Into a mirror

This will crack with the intensity of stares.


Who will gather

Those fragments?

**Returning.**

Returning from a father's anger,

Returning from a mother womb,

Returning from sperm and egg,

Returning from parent's ecstasy.


Returning from the Crucifixion,

Returning from the Incarnation,

Returning from Buddha Nirvana,

Returning from Creation's Bang,


From Nothingness to Existence.

**This is How it Was.**

Patriotic parents without lungs who breathed through gills,

They were waving flags without intact minds sunset bodies,

A smiling lesbian strolling with false residence documents,

Tombstone Trotskyists with the glint of cold steel in the eye,

Anarchists glare and sell their copy of fortnightly *'Freedom'*,

Situationist sisters and brothers with cracked petrol bombs,

Dreamers who had forgotten their dreams and visions died,

All stumble through an unmarked minefield risk mutilation,

Mallet headed secret police intertwining quietly listening,

Progressive priests pardon sin and pick-up an ArmaLite,

Lover's countdown to lose an illusory pleasure in the flesh,

Their bodies in a tumbling tangle of sensations and touch,

Rooms heaving with the bilious smoke of hashish smoked,

Some syringes with congealed blood on threadbare mats,

Group-therapists waging war on the Little-Ones, we resist.

**On the Scene.**

Look whose back on the Scene man,

Lay some dope on him, be cool man,

A little acid tune him to the frequency

Give some speed to wake-up a brain,

Do- him- up with smack to get a habit,

Look whose back on the Scene man,

O.D. Off the scene is blue he is dead.

**Breakdown: seeing beyond.**

Seeing beyond the tokens of things,

To just penetrate the masks of men,

And to lift the veils of woman reveal,

Looking beyond a child's tears, sobs,

To see a screaming devouring mouth,

It could rip a communicant from wine,

Hurling them all into a Dantesque fire,

Of forgotten selves and dream ghosts,

Who roam the ploughed, frosty fields?

There she glistens in that lunar- sea,

Will she melt in the winter sunshine?

**The 'Man', the dealer**

You, grooving along an undulating pathway,

Streetlights cannot penetrate that darkness,

Visiting The Man as he has good gear I hear,

I duck down the alleyway at last in the temple,

A face of friendship greets, I pay £20, 2 bags,

Weeping in the shooting-gallery with friends,

Brown sugar and she twinkles into the spoon,

He rubs up our tubes until are ulcerated pipes,

Wham thank you Man, I fall into the cushions.

**One.**

That slimy silence is just deafening,

The Void, pregnant with a meaning,

We, I, and all the People in my head,

Are mirrors of all potential  Pathways,

Through chaos and the atoms of self,

A social consciousness is just isolation,

Strangled by the honeysuckle of lover's

Woven nets, a betrayal of the revolution.

**Two.**

A baby is weeping in a storm cloud,

A prisoner on the rack is screaming,

The parents rock to a belted climax,

Another baby born into The Inferno,

And the parents beat their breasts.

Nigel Pearce

**Three**

A tempest crested wave crashed on his shore,

Like the rhythms of the sea eroding a coastline,

Suddenly his body is flung up into a blazing sky,

Soaring with swallows on the wind's wild current,

Aware of the finite with the sea and its roof of sky,

Only to embrace the hummed Mass in his cranium,

Police came and smashed, crashed down a door,

He, a swaying cornfield routed the thought-police,

To recruit them to the revolutionary proletariat aim,

A sea is bashing his mind until free he flies away.

**Five.**

I, like a chick who is emerging from an egg,

Wanting not to be born, it has been ordained,

In this farmyard with that choking dust blown,

He, she, they are all pecking around for corn,

Just to survive to exist in this yard that is hard,

The farmer does not feed us chicks properly.


Farmers will not let these to live as they wish,

For this is the generation of the battery-hens.

**Seven.**

Still yet a living frame without a soul,

A fire ignited by the Earth's pulsations,

Lost youth travelled in a zigzag tonight,

Still trapped in a maze yelling for help,

A man is caught in the breeze, no farm,

Only the Owner within ploughs his field.

**Eleven.**

The memories return in the asylum with breakdown trough,

As when a woman lies with her newborn, no father to be seen,

I wander through fields of gold swaying corn and think of snow,

But Mozart stepped across the terrain of the self and the universe.

**Twelve**

The Radical Feminist sees the baton-wielding policeman in every

man. She may not perceive so readily the crying baby son who is

also present, hidden by Patriarchy. As a system of ideas she does

understand the system the Male Law-Giver wrote, imposed upon

those Tablets of Stone, but not those men crucified by those Laws.

**SHE.**

Woman is the manna on the breeze,

Woman is the wind that plays chimes,

The hands that play and stroke a harp,

They welcome like warmth, shy, sharp,

Respond with moonbeams on the lips,

The memories conjoined never separate,

She is the stream entering green oceans.

**She mutilates the Temple of Her Body.**

My body has become a twisted shrine,

Is a tube of paste that is oozing slime,

It must be cut to allow the pus to flow,

The knife straight blade purges wrath,

This is incense to be inhaled by them,

Intoxicate them like a cyanide pellet,

She, the ultimate soliloquist departs.

**A warm woman and a cold girl.**

Grooving along a cold pavement,

Taking poems to a warm woman,

Cold girl just leers across a street,

With her harsh stems of corn hair,

Her eyes are dead, she is an advert,

Those ruby lips, mouth something,

A shallowness of mass magazines,

Not like a flowing river-fire woman,

Who reads and writes lunar poetry.

Nigel Pearce

### Today.

The poets languish in the mental hospitals,

The criminals are running the government,

The poor live in concrete boxes or streets,

Mind-control priests celebrating the Mass,

We weep from bruised, blackened red eyes.

**Before the Incense was lit.**

Before they lit their choking Incense,

He was

Dammed before the beginning of Time,

Fated to shed tears like autumn leaves,

Cursed to be blown by the hurricane,

Doomed to be drenched in raged rain

Blighted at birth to be a series of selves.


A temple has been desecrated by fools,

Even before incense was burning scent,

At the Farwell, let there be no lamentation.

**No Path.**

Those stagnant pool parents,

Who only raged at innocents?

Inhaled choking smoking fog,

Which they breathed as Jews,

In cyanide shower death camp.

They had only a death-in-death,

Not understanding a path obscure.


In which water rhythmically washes

Away the grains of sun, moon sands,

But falling in a void visions and voices,

This was beyond Reason like a dream,

Until he agreed with heart quite smashed,

To wander quiet in the twilight zone alone.

**Hermaphrodite Kiss.**

He had wept as the nappy-pin japed him,

He had hidden behind sofas feared at six,

He found shelter in a syringe and bottle, 12.


The Minotaur had roared without any control,

Careered through the labyrinth stabbing horn,


Like a twinkling moth he

                    Immolated on flames,

Adoring the collapse of his veins and stigmata,

Choreology in the darkest oceans of the moon.


We mutants offer a hermaphrodite midnight kiss.

Nigel Pearce

**Families**

Families are places where the ghosts roam,

The spectres are screeching with each other,

The walls of this home dissolve in nightmares,

Those gales just howl through, blown all over,

The gales howl like the wolves that were here,

A child shakes wite pain and the clenched fear.

**Sleeplessness.**

Walking through these cold nights of bitter sleeplessness,

My being slid down the dustpipe, a Way of Nothingnees,

Images become distorted in a mirror of caustic Absurdity,

These are both within and without no escape they shout.


Will any kink of peace, wipe my clay body, feverish brow,

Will the whisky-bottle or the syringe be a cloth of comfort,

Just to hush, hush this chaos that burns like hell in mind,

And dissolve the sou to stop the cancer eating my body.


This barrenness of spirit with the potency of emotions,

They cut like a missed arrow of love pierces the heart,

Lead to a desired death or a wilted bed of rose petals.

**Mirrors.**

They are no mirrors,

They are not in others,

They are not in my eyes,

Or in my soul or on the desk,

Not in parents,

Not in children,

A cloud of tears which will not rain,

Shattered all mirrors when it hailed,

Upon the winter windows of childhood.

**No walls, no floor.**

There were no walls of haven in a family,

And certainly there was no heaven ceiling,

No solid earth floor to stand upon or walk,

It was sub-terrain world of misty shadow,

It would with certainty of sunset explode,

A fiendish and hellish land of like Inferno,

Where all were tormented by their demons,

A family where no family ever could coexist,

I was born no self, a *Tabula rasa* smashed.

**Inside my Skull.**

Within the cave of one mind,

The skull of Dante's disciple,

Roam two evil men, who shout,

They both accuse he of devilry,

One contorted group therapist,

One a policeman with a baton,

They are stones within a soul,

They are beyond an exorcism.

**Angie.**

She has worn a blue wool dress besmirched with coffee stains. Buttressed against the cold and the World with jumpers and a belief in witchcraft. She hummed with delight and rose coloured blushes when her breasts were caressed with holy lips of a prophet,. Her heaven roamed across her flesh as his tongue darted and teeth nipped. Only to drown in a sea of esotoretic sighs. I loved her with my soul, relished her body if not the mind, I had lost mine. We twinkled across the fields in the moonlight. Until consumed we lay and slept in reveries. The police found a poet in a graveyard one frosty night, he was insane and awaiting a Resurrection of the Dead.

### Eclipses.

Her mind whispered with firm gentleness emphasising words,

And his cerebral activity was transformed visions caught eyes.

He travelled beyond choking orbits to the dark side of the moon,

At dawn awaits, but is forgotten, it is solitude that like jail contains.

He is kissed by squiggling so back to my 'script' chamber maid 'me'

He had his fill of her. I attain the apotheosis a lonely outcast knows.

**Some Final Thoughts on the nature of altered consciousness.**

During my thesis I will attempt to answer the question of whether religious belief can be used to justify belief in God by employing the method of deductive logic. I shall place this 'argument' in the context of two competing views of religious experience, firstly William James, who perceived it as generally positive, but then deploy Jean-Paul Sartre's counterargument of 'bad faith' . I shall use a 'thought-experiment' of my own devising to illustrate my positions. The 'argument' itself is similar to that of David Hume (1990 [1779]) and in the tradition of British Empiricism questions any form of a priori 'truth from authority' and therefore I utilise a methodology which originates in Hume who I employ and quote but also attempt to make it contemporary using examples from Kierkegaard, Swinburne, Engels and Marx. After my 'argument' has concluded that religious experiences do occur, but are contrary to the laws of the natural world and are rather the projected essence of an alienated humanity. I conclude with the protagonist of the 'thought-experiment' achieving an Aristotelian sense of eudemonia. Therefore, firstly I would like to examine two 20th century responses to religious experience, its relationship to self and others and the consequences of the respective positions in regard of these experiences of God. I shall here suggest that the ramifications of the perspectives has a very contemporary resonance, i.e. how do people behave 'authentically' in response to a religious experience of a Deity or 'Higher Power'. The contrast will be illustrated by a 'thought-experiment'. The term 'religious experience' is used quite loosely in William James (1902) The Varieties of Religious Experience. He defined this experience as a 'proof' but not in the way contemporary Catholic theologian Alasdair Macintyre does when he argued: 'Truth is tradition- constituted' (Chappell, 2011 p.151) for a particular religion. Rather for James the 'sign' of genuine religious experience was a generalized 'moral proof' rather than embracing a particular tradition. At broadly transformative experience which leads to a state of consciousness in which:

'...one aim grows so stable as to expel definitively its previous rivals from the individual life.'

James (1902), Lecture IX p, 191.

A 'thought-experiment' could be an alcoholic going on the programme prescribed by Alcoholics Anonymous and embracing a 'Higher Power' as a solution to their addiction and thereby facilitating a personal and moral transformation. They may be deceived and deceiving as a result of this experience of the Divine. The 'onus of proof' is with those advocating the 'salvation' of my subject to the detriment of their human authenticity. Jean-Paul Sartre uses a term, 'bad faith'. Sartre defines 'bad faith' as a hiding of truth from self, an inauthenticity in the face of existential reality which is absurd because there is no Deity, following Nietzsche and 'the death of God' (Nietzsche (1882 [1977] ) The Gay Science, Section 125). Paradoxically, for Sartre to belief in 'bad faith' one must belief it to be true, it becomes dialectical, the victim is both the perpetrator of the deception yet also its victim because it denies him or her existential 'freedom' So at the same time the liar, as liar, believes the lie to be false, and as a victim believes it to be true. So there is a contradiction in that when a person acts in 'bad faith' or self-deception believes something to be true and false at the same time. In Being and Nothingness (1976) he writes:

'Thus in order for bad faith to be possible, sincerity itself must be bad faith'

Sartre (1976) p 67

To illustrate this Sartre uses a 'thought- experiment' of a waiter who is too eager to please:

'(as he carries the food) his movement is quick and forward, a little too precise, a little too rapid.'

Sartre (1993), pp. 167-169.

To return to my 'thought-experiment', the alcoholic may believe in God or a 'Higher Power' but their zealousness may, if Sartre is correct and I think he is, reveal that they have deceived themselves, and because of the interdependent unity of opposites in dialectical formulations, others as well. I would suggest that the first position in my 'thought-experiment' is based on an enthymeme, the unstated assumption or premise being that the religious experience is necessary beneficial and that for the alcoholic to deceive themself and others is therefore simply a non sequitur, it 'does not follow'. Having explored the nature of the religious perspective from these two contrasting perspectives I shall embark on the argument by using deductive logic as understood here:

'Logic may be defined as the theory of the conditions of valid inference, or more shortly, as the theory of proof. Inference is a process by which we pass from a belief in one or more statements (the premises) to a belief in a further statement (the conclusion) whose truth, if the inference is a good one, is either guaranteed or at least made probable by the truth of the premises.'

Ree and Ormson (ed), (2005) p.211.

Hence the basic structure of my argument will be as follows:

Premise 1: A religious experience is transcendent and caused by a Divine Being, it is subjective. But it is not a hallucination.

Premise 2: The material world exists and is governed by objective laws.

Subconclusion 1: So if people have subjective experiences of God these necessary transcend or 'violate' the material world and its laws.

Premise 3: All that exists is this material world is governed by its own laws and is not transformed by the intervention of a Divine Being.

Subconclusion 2: So religious experiences are created by a transcendental God intervening in the world and are not caused by the laws of the material world.

Premise 4: As all that exists is the material world and is caused by that physical world therefore religious experiences are illusions.

Conclusion: Therefore, because religious experiences are based on illusions they can be used to justify a belief in God who cannot intervene in the material world because the Deity it is an illusion or a projection and thus it follows that objectively God does not exist.

It is necessary to contrast Natural Theology, which maintains that knowledge of the Divine can be achieved through Reason and observation of the world, as in the teleological argument, in order to ascertain the existence of the Deity and another branch of the philosophy of religion which is founded in Revelation and seeks knowledge of Divinity in miracles and sacred scripture. A reliance on the later leads to fideism or a belief in 'justification by faith alone' and possibly found its highest manifestation in the philosophy of Kierkegaard who argued that people must simply make 'a leap of faith' this I would argue is another example of Sartre's 'bad faith'.

However Natural Theology and Revelation are not mutually exclusive and it in the area of miracles and religious experience they overlap and interact. The key issue is Evidentialism in that it is necessary to define what evidence is appropriate to make a claim for a proof of a miracle and more pertinently to this thesis 'religious experience'. The counter argument to Evidentialism is made by Revelation 'No one has ever seen God' (John 1:18) [1962]. However, following Hume I argue in a similar vein to him:

'The plain consequence is (and it is a general maxim worthy of our attention)

'That no testimony is sufficient to establish a miracle, unless the testimony be of such kind that its falsehood would be more miraculous than the fact which it attempts to follow.'

Hume (1748) in Cottingham p 373.

Firstly, as Swinburne argues:

If it seems to me that I have a glimpse of Heaven, or a vision of God that is grounds for me and others to suppose I have.'

Swinburne (1968) pp. 320-328.

So here we have an experience of a supernatural being or entity being experienced by a Fellow of the British Academy and therefore we may presume it is not a hallucination and he is sane.

Secondly we have an account of a material world that is governed by objective laws. Engels presents the argument:

'the great basic question of all philosophy... is that of thinking to being

...Thus the question of the relation of thinking to being, the relation of the spirit to nature is the paramount religious question.'

Engels (1975) pp13-14.

Maurice Cornforth reinforces two points:

1. Materialism teaches that the world is by its very nature material that everything which exists comes into being on the basis of material causes, rises and develops in accordance with the laws of matter.

2. Materialism teaches that matter is objective reality existing outside and independent of the mind; and that far from the mental existing in separation from the material, everything mental or spiritual is the product of material processes.

   Cornforth (1977) p 25.

Therefore I have established the first premise:

1) That religious experience exists in a definable sense and the second, a position for a material analysis of reality.

Hence the Subconclusion inferred from these is that if religious experience exists it must violate the laws of the material world in the same way Hume says a miracle:

'May be accurately defined, a transgression of the law of nature by a particular violation of the Deity, or by the interposition of some invisible agent.'

Hume (2000) p.87.

It must be experienced subjectively but not be a product of insanity it must also be accompanied by a 'sense' of the Divine which is verifiable by other member of the person's culture.

Premise 3 is defined by Cornforth (1977) p.27

Materialism teaches that the world and its laws are knowable, and that while much in the material world may not be known there is no sphere of reality which lies outside of the material world. Marxist philosophy is characterised by it's absolutely consistently materialism.'

Thus I arrive at a second Subconclusion here inferred from above that if religious experience exists and cannot be the product of the material world then it must be derived from a transcendental being revealed by revelation.

My fourth premise is articulated by Marx:

'Religion is the sigh of the oppressed creature... It is the opium of the people. The abolition of religion as the illusory happiness of the people is the demand for their real happiness. To call on them to give up their illusions about their condition is to call on them to give up a condition that requires illusions.'

Marx. (1975). p2

My argument is essentially that religious experiences are illusory and a product of alienation.

This lead to my conclusion that if religious experiences occur which they do and the world is governed by material laws which it is, then these experiences must be illusions and by extrapolation God is a delusion, a product of an alienated humanity 'projecting' its essence or what the young Marx called it 'species-being' into the heavens.

In the 'thought experiment' my alcoholic subject may have had a religious experience through a 'Higher Power' and conquered his addiction, but after meeting a existentialist philosophy student who introduced him to Sartre starts drinking again but lives 'authentically'. He then goes through a 'dry' spell and has a 'genuine' spiritual experience and decides to work in a shelter for the homeless. Here he meets an old man who introduces him to Marxist philosophy. He then realizes that he was alienated from his 'true' humanity, joins a revolutionary group in order to attempt to transform the social conditions that give rise to illusions such as religion. He finally as an old man is content after reading Aristotle on eudemon.

The argument is although people have religious experiences, they paradoxically disproof a Divinity by their illusionary nature. That a fideism based on Kierkegaard or a claim to 'justification by faith alone' must disprove what it attempts to prove. Natural theology is more balanced, but its argument from analogy requires if not a 'leap of faith' too far but too great a leap of logic. The solution, I suggest, lies in this method outlined here by Marx:

> The foundation of irreligious criticism is: *Man makes religion*, religion
> does not make man. Religion is, indeed, the self-consciousness
> and self-esteem of man who has either not yet won through to himself, or
> has already lost himself again. But *man* is no abstract being squatting
> outside the world. Man is *the world of man* – state, society. This state
> and this society produce religion, which is an *inverted consciousness*
> *of the world*, because they are an *inverted world*. Religion is the general
> theory of this world, its encyclopaedic compendium, its logic in popular form,

its spiritual *point d'honneur*, its enthusiasm, its moral sanction, its solemn complement, and its universal basis of consolation and justification. It is the *fantastic realization* of the human essence since the human *essence* has not acquired any true reality. The struggle against religion is, therefore, indirectly the struggle *against that world* whose spiritual *aroma* is religion. Religious suffering is, at one and the same time, the expression of real suffering and a protest against real suffering. Religion is the sigh of the oppressed creature, the heart of a heartless world, and the soul of soulless conditions. It is the opium of the people. The abolition of religion as the illusory happiness of the people is the demand for their real happiness. To call on them to give up their illusions ut their condition is to call on them to give up a condition that requires illusions. The criticism of religion is, therefore, in embryo, the criticism of that vale of tears of which religion is the halo. Criticism has plucked the imaginary flowers on the chain not in order that man shall continue to bear that chain without fantasy or consolation, but so that he shall throw off the chain and pluck the living flower. The criticism of religion disillusions man, so that he will think, act, and fashion his reality like a man who has discarded his illusions and regained his senses, so that he will move around himself as his own true Sun. Religion is only the illusory Sun which revolves around man as long as he does not revolve around himself.

- Marx (1975) pp. 1-2..

My hope is the Flight of Icarus was not in vain, we did not bring down the patriarchal capitalist monolith, but as I was determined my experience would not be banal. That it would smudge the dividing line between literature and everyday life.

**Bibliography.**

Bible (1962) *Revised Standard Version*, American Bible Society.

Chappell, T (2011) *The Philosophy of Religion*, Exploring Philosophy, Milton Keynes, The Open University.

Cornforth, M (1977) *Materialism and the Dialectical Method*, London, Lawrence and Wishart.

Cottingham, J (ed) (2008) *Western Philosophy: An Anthology*, Blackwell Publishing.

Davies, B (2004*) An Introduction To The Philosophy Of Religion*, New York, Oxford University Press.

Engels, F (1975) *Ludwig Feuerbach and the End of Classical German Philosophy,* Moscow, Progress Publishers.

Hume, D (2000) (Ed) Tom. L. Beauchamp, *An Enquiry concerning Human Understanding*, New York, Oxford University Press.

Hume, D (1990 [1776*]) Discourses concerning Natural Religion* (ed Martin Bell), London, Penguin Classics

James, W (1902) *The Varieties of Religious Experience*, New York, Modern Library.

Marx, K (1975) *Contribution to the Critique of Hegel's Philosophy of Law*, Moscow, Progress Publishers.

Ree, J and Urmson, O.R (ed) (2005) *The Concise Encyclopaedia of Western Philosophy*, New York, Routledge.

Nietzsche, F (1977(1882]) *A Nietzsche Reader*, (ed) R.J.Hollingdale, London, Penguin Classics.

Sartre, J, P (1976) *Being and Nothingness*, London, Methuen & Co Ltd.

Sartre, J.P (1993) *Essays in Existentialism*, New York, Citadel Press.

Swinburne, R (1968) 'Miracles', Philosophy Quarterly. *Philosophical Quarterly 18 (73)*.

www.ingramcontent.com/pod-product-compliance
Lightning Source LLC
Chambersburg PA
CBHW022132080426
42734CB00006B/330